P9-ASM-453

HOW FAITH WORKS

Revised and Expanded

by
Dr. Frederick K.C. Price

Harrison House
Tulsa, Oklahoma

Unless otherwise indicated, all Scripture quotations are taken from *The New King James Version,* copyright © 1979, 1980, 1982, Thomas Nelson, Inc.

Scripture quotations marked (KJV) are taken from the *King James Version* of the Bible.

Scripture quotations marked Weymouth are taken from *The New Testament in Modern Speech* by Richard Francis Weymouth. Copyright © 1978 by Kregel Publications, Grand Rapids, Michigan.

Scripture quotations marked AMP are taken from *The Amplified Bible, New Testament.* Copyright © 1958, 1987 by the Lockman Foundation, La Habra, California. Used by permission.

Verses marked (TLB) are taken from *The Living Bible* © 1971. Used by permission of Tyndale House Publishers, Inc., Wheaton, Illinois 60189. All rights reserved.

Direct quotations from Scripture are in bold face type.

5th Printing

How Faith Works:
Revised and Expanded
(Formerly ISBN 0-89274-001-9)
ISBN 0-89274-975-X
Copyright © 1976, 1996 by Frederick K.C. Price, Ph.D.
Crenshaw Christian Center
P. O. Box 90000
Los Angeles, California 90009

Published by Harrison House, Inc.
P. O. Box 35035
Tulsa, Oklahoma 74153

Printed in the United States of America. All rights reserved under International Copyright Law. Contents and/or cover may not be reproduced in whole or in part in any form without the express written consent of the Publisher.

Contents

PART I

FAITH AND BELIEF:
ARE THEY THE SAME?

1

The Importance of Faith

The very first thing that I want to do is to establish the importance of faith. I am firmly convinced that the most important subject for a person to learn—after they are born again—is how to walk by faith. Nothing is more important than learning to walk by faith. That is my personal opinion.

You cannot convince me that anything is more important than faith. Because if you think you know of something, I will be able to prove to you that faith is more important than that.

I do not mean faith is more important to the exclusion and the total dismissal of other spiritual things, as though they are not important, But, rather, I am talking about *priority*. I am talking about the fact that it is *the* number one *priority*, in sequence to other things.

Faith Versus Love

Someone may say, "Love is the most important thing." But allow me to show you that faith is more important than love. I am not saying that faith *takes the place of love*. (Keep in mind that I am dealing with priority.) You need to learn about faith *before* you learn about love. And the reason you need to do that is because you are going to have to learn how to love people *by faith*.

If you do not have faith and you do not know how to operate in it, you are not going to be able to love. You might say, "Oh, Brother Price, I disagree with that, because it is very clearly revealed in First Corinthians 13:13:

> **And now abide faith, hope, love, these three; but the greatest of these is love.**

In reading that passage of Scripture, you might think it contradicts what I said about faith being a priority. But you need to understand what you are reading.

Scripture Must Be Read in Context

The problem is that people have taken that last part of First Corinthians 13 and extracted it from its setting and used it as a principle. They interpret it as saying, *love is more important than anything else*. However, that is not what Paul is writing about. To understand it in context, you have to read chapter 12 and chapter 14.

To help you understand, let me clarify the setting: there were problems in the church at Corinth in terms of the people not understanding fully how to operate in the things of the Spirit. As a result, there was confusion and misunderstanding. Therefore, the Body at Corinth was not being edified as it could have been edified if they had understood how to flow in the Spirit. So Paul inserted First Corinthians 13, right between chapters 12 and 14, to show the people that in order to operate in chapters 12 and 14, they should do it out of a motive of "love."

Love Is the Greatest Motivator

Love is the greatest motivator—the primary motive by which one should do anything. There is no greater motivator than "love." In other words, I ought to serve God because I love Him. I ought to pay my tithes because I love God. I ought to live right because I love God. I ought to read the Word, study the Word and pray because of a motive of love. I ought to give to my brothers and sisters, I ought to lay hands on the sick, because I love.

I should not lay hands on the sick to show how powerful a man of faith I am—to get the person healed, then stand back and gloat saying, "Oh, look at me! I'm really something special! I got this person healed!" I should be ministering to the person out of a motive of love.

That is what Paul was talking about. When it comes to the motivator, **...and now abide faith, hope, love...** the greatest motivator is love. I should not be motivated just because I have faith. I should be moved or motivated because I have love.

Faith Is the Activator

Let me share a principle: *Love is the **motivator**, but faith is the **activator**.*

Galatians 5:6 says, **faith *working through* love**. What does that mean? That is the motive by which your faith ought to operate. However, we are not talking about the motive right now. We are talking about the *activator*, which is faith. That is why faith is more important than love.

It is more important than love because you actually cannot love people unless you love them by faith. In order to love people as brothers and sisters in Christ, you have to love them by faith.

Yes, faith does work by a motive of love, but I have news for you: even though it is not written, *love works by faith*. Just stop and think about it. You all have relatives, friends, people you work with and people you know who are hard to love. There are some people who are even hard to *like*! Forget trying to love them!

In such cases, if you do not know how to operate by faith, you will have challenges. And that is why some of you have challenges interacting with other Christian brethren.

All of us have our special personalities. Most of the time, you try to be yourself, but you do not always come off right with other people. Other people do not always perceive you the way you want to present yourself. For example, some people perceive me as arrogant, simply because I am confident. Simply because I know who I am in Christ. Simply because I am delivered. Simply because I have a purpose in mind and I know what I was called to do, and what God wants me to do.

Many people consider that as arrogance, because most people are so *namby-pamby* and *wishy-washy* and have such low self-esteem that they are afraid to be that bold. But that is just my personality and it has nothing to do with what arrogance really means.

I often talk about material matters because everyone can relate to the material matters of life. I use such things to focus on a point, not because I am materialistic. People write letters and say, "You're too materialistic!" But that is only their *perception* of me. We all perceive one another in different ways.

Nevertheless, someone might have a problem loving me just because *they* think I am arrogant and materialistic. But you have to learn to love me by faith, just like I have to learn to love you by faith.

You Must Relate To Others by Faith

You have to learn how to relate to people by faith. That is why I said it is more important than love. I did not say it was the only thing or that you should not have love. But if you do not know how to operate by faith, then you are going to have a hard time relating to other brothers and sisters in the Body of Christ.

Sometimes you might get into close encounters with individuals, maybe in the Body of Christ or in some church setting, and it is just like rubbing up against sandpaper. You get to the point where you don't want to talk to that person.

In fact, you don't want to see them because you don't have an emotional feeling of even liking them. But you have to get beyond that.

I should not relate to you because I have a feeling or an emotion. I have to do it because God said so. We are commanded to love one another. And if I love you, then I have to treat you right. But your attitude is so ugly, I cannot get past it. Do you know what I mean? So in an instance like that, I have to do it by faith. That is why I say faith is so important.

Obedience Is by Faith

Someone may say, "Obedience is more important than faith." But how can you be obedient without faith? You have to operate by faith in order to be obedient.

Let's talk about tithing for instance. You have to operate by faith to give away 10 percent of your income. There is no way you are going to give away 10 percent of your income to a God you cannot see, unless you know *how faith works!*

What About Prayer?

Someone says, "What about prayer?" *Prayer?* How do you know a God you cannot see is going to answer what you just asked? How do you know God heard you? Well, of course His Word says so, but you have to have faith in His Word to believe that He is there, and that He will hear you and answer you. So you have to have faith.

Everything in the Kingdom of God is going to be activated and accessed by your faith. That is why it is so important.

Definitions Bring Understanding

In order for us to discuss and analyze the subject of *how faith works*, I need to give you some definitions. In other words, we need to define our terms. Our first definition is the word, *faith:* Greek, *(pistis);* "persuasion, i.e., credence, moral conviction (of religious truth, or the truthfulness of God or a religious teacher), especially reliance upon Christ for salvation; abstractly [meaning] constancy in such profession; by extension the system of religious (Gospel) truth itself..." [For instance, someone says: "What *faith* are you, Protestant, Catholic, or Jew?"] "...assurance, belief, believe, faith, fidelity."[1]

Our second definition is the word, *believe:* Greek, *(pisteuo);* "to have faith (in, upon, or with respect to, a person or thing), i.e., credit; by implication, to entrust (especially one's spiritual well-being to Christ): - believe (-r), commit (to trust), put in trust with."[2]

You will notice that the definitions of *faith* and *believe* are basically the same. But in actuality, I want to propose to you that the difference between faith and belief is as far as the earth is from the sun, which is 93 million miles.

---

[1]James Strong, "Greek Dictionary of the New Testament," *The New Strong's Exhaustive Concordance of the Bible,* (Nashville: Thomas Nelson Publishers, 1984), p. 58, #4102.

[2]New Strong's, "Greek Dictionary," p. 58, #4100.

2

Faith and Belief Are Different

I believe there is a tremendous difference between faith and belief, and you need to understand that difference. The first thing I want to do is to show you the difference by illustration between faith and belief. Then I want to give you my definition of faith and then give you Scriptures to validate my definition and let you be the judge as to whether or not my definition of faith is a valid definition that you can agree with.

I want to show you the difference between two words. But first of all, let me ask you a question: have you ever heard the word *faith*? Have you ever heard the words *belief, believe, believer* or *believing*?

Now, for another question: have you taken for granted that *faith* and *belief* are basically the same thing — just two different ways of saying the same thing? For example, I could say, *woman, female* and *mother*. Those are different designations, and of course, there are some actual differences. But if I said *woman, female,* or *mother,* you would not think of a male pig. You would think of the helpmate that God said Adam needed, right? *Woman.* Yet you could use those words interchangeably.

So, have you, perhaps, thought that *faith* and *belief* were just another way of saying *female* and *woman?* In other words, you might have thought they were basically the same thing. If you're talking about faith, you are talking about belief. And if you are talking about belief, you are talking about faith. That thinking process can be a great deterrent to your operating in the fullness of God. I want to illustrate this by an object lesson.

Faith and Belief Are Two Sides of the Same Coin

I say there is a difference between faith and belief in actual everyday living, and that difference is astronomical. If you do not know and understand the difference, you can think that you are operating in faith when in fact all you will be doing is believing. You will see the difference by a graphic illustration.

Visualize that I have in my hand a twenty-five cent piece. It is referred to as a quarter, or one-fourth of a dollar. This coin has been minted or authorized to be made and distributed by the United States Treasury. It is considered legal tender, meaning this coin can be traded on the open economic market for goods and services.

This coin on one side has an emblem stamped on it. This particular emblem is the head of our first President of the United States, George Washington. That particular *side* is usually referred to in common street talk as the heads side of the coin. On the opposite side of the coin, there is an eagle with his wings outstretched, which is the federal bird of the federal republic of the United States of America. And that side of the coin is usually referred to as the tails side. Heads and tails.

Again, this coin is considered legal tender. However, there is a stipulation that both sides of the coin have to be intact in order to be spendable. If I were to take this coin into a machine shop, put it in a vice grip, put it on a grinding wheel and grind off the president's head so that it is just a shiny piece of metal with no head, or emblem on it, a merchant or salesperson is under no obligation to accept the coin as legal tender, because it is now defaced.

Both sides of the coin have to be intact in order for the coin to spend on the open economic market. If you look at this coin, there is a vast difference between the eagle and George Washington.

Now, I submit to you that in God's open spiritual market, God also has legal tender. He has a coin that will spend on the open spiritual market. You can trade it for goods and services. That coin has two sides. But you have to have both sides intact in order for the coin to spend. One side is faith, and one side is belief. The difference between faith and belief is just as different as the president's head and the eagle on a twenty-five cent piece.

Faith and Belief Must Work Together

Let me show you by illustration that there is truly a difference between faith and belief. Let us say that while I am speaking in the FaithDome someone walks through the door and comes down the aisle. Everyone is intent on what I am saying and not really watching anything else. Suddenly this man appears right up front. You look at this man. He looks strange. He is very emaciated, sickly, and very weak looking. In fact, he looks just like death going somewhere to happen. He looks bad. He looks starved.

He walks up to the platform. We are all amazed at his audacity. Everyone is spellbound. He walks on the platform and goes to the podium. He raises his hand to get the attention of everyone and begins to say, "Ladies and gentlemen, I uh,uh,uh...." and he falls over backwards flat on the floor.

The ushers rush forward to see if they can revive him. The head usher goes to the microphone and says, "Do we have a doctor in the house?" And by chance there is. He just happens to have his little black medical bag with him. He walks on the stage to examine this man. By this time we have the man stretched out on the platform.

After examining the man, the doctor goes to the microphone and says, "Ladies and gentlemen, we need to pray or do something, because this man is in the final stages of starvation. He is so undernourished, so anemic, so lacking nutrition that given another thirty minutes, if he doesn't eat he will die. He is that far gone. It is indeed a bad situation."

Someone says, "We will send over to the cafeteria and get some food."

Within minutes, the cafeteria workers come down the aisle pushing this little white cart. On this cart are all kinds of delectable goodies, guaranteed to satisfy the most discriminating palate. By this time, the man has been revived and is sitting on a chair. Everyone is watching. The cafeteria workers bring the cart loaded with food and wheel it right up in front of him. I come to the man and say, "Sir, may I ask you a question?" He says, "Yes, you may."

I say, "Sir, do you believe that if you eat this food, it will keep you from starving to death?" And almost with indignity he replies, "Do you think I am some kind of fool? Do you think that I am stupid or dumb by some chance? Do you think I am some kind of ignoramus? Certainly I believe that if I eat this food, it will keep me from starving to death."

Now remember the doctor's prognosis—thirty minutes maximum, if this man doesn't eat, he is going to die. The man is in bad shape. Do you have this picture? So, twenty-nine minutes and fifty-four seconds later, the man is heard to say, "I believe that if I eat this food, it will keep me from starving to death. I absolutely, positively believe that if I eat this food, it will definitely keep me from starving to death...." And he plunges out of the chair onto the floor.

The doctor rushes up to his side and examines him, turns to the audience and says, "Ladies and gentlemen, this man is dead."

Now, I want to ask a question, and this is not a trick question. It is not designed to put you on the spot. And don't try to be cool about it. Be honest about your answer. Because this illustration can only help you.

Many people think they know what it is to walk by faith, and it is very obvious if you examine their lives very carefully, they do not know that they do not know. And sometimes someone who does not know they do not know is the hardest person in the world to get the point across to, because they *think* they know.

You read the whole scenario. Here is the question: would you be honest enough to say that what the man *said* he believed was absolutely true? Would you say that what the man said he *believed* was definitely not true? Or, would you have to say at this point, "Dr. Price, to be absolutely honest with you, I am not really sure."

Here is what is interesting about this situation. Whenever I ask these three questions, I always get three answers.

We have all read the same story about the same man, yet we come up with three different answers. Confusing? You think I don't need to teach on this? I do! First of all, I will tell you why you said you are not sure. You figured if what the man believed was true, he would not have died. "But since he died, I do not know." That is what you are thinking or saying.

Those who said that what the man believed was true, were accurate. The ones who said it was not true thought that because they assumed if it were true, the man would have lived. But, according to summation, since he died, it must not be true.

Faith Is Acting on What You Believe

Actually, what the man believed was absolutely, positively, unequivocally, historically, and scientifically true. Everything he believed was true. If he had eaten that food, he would not have died. But he died. Now why did he die? Because he did not eat. *The eating is the faith part.* Definition: *faith is acting on what you believe.* You will not find this in *Vine's* or *Young's Concordance* or any Greek dictionary.

Faith is acting on what you believe. If you do not act on it, though what you believe is true, it will not change your circumstances. The man died. Yet you could not find one thing wrong with his believing. Everything he believed was absolutely true. But it did him no good. You know why? *Because he did not act on it.* Faith is acting on what you believe.

Believing something will never change your circumstances, but *faith* will change your circumstances. And faith is acting on what you believe.

Believing is where you start. But if all you do is believe, there will be no life-changing results forthcoming. That is why so many Christians throughout the years have been destroyed by Satan. They believe God *can* heal, and yet they are dying like flies.

Their believing is right. *The man said,* "I believe if I eat the food it will keep me from starving to death." Yet he died, starved, with food in front of him. Why? He never ate it. He never acted on his belief. You are not going to get healed because God *can* heal. You have to find out what it takes to get God's *can* into God's *will.*

You can go to the local supermarket, get a market basket, walk down every aisle of the supermarket. Fill the basket with so much food you cannot see past the pile of food. You can wheel that basket into the center aisle of the supermarket and cry out as loud as you can, "I believe that if I eat this food it will keep me from starving to death."

Everything you believe is absolutely true. But you can die right in the center aisle of the local supermarket, with all that food in the basket and your hands on the basket— unless you get the food out of the basket and into you. *Believing is right, but it will not change the circumstances.*

Believing Is the Starting Point

Believing is where you start, but if that is where you stop, you will get nothing for the believing. Can you understand that? It is so important to understand that difference.

Think about it: do you have the keys to a car you own? Put this book down, go to the place where your car is parked, climb up on the hood of your car and hold your keys up for everyone to see and say, "I believe that if I get in my car, put these keys in the ignition, turn it on, my car will start. I can put it in gear and drive someplace." However, you will be standing on the hood of that car until hell freezes over unless you get off the hood, get in the car, put the key in, turn it on, start the car, put it in gear and drive some place.

Everything you believed was absolutely true—but you will only leave that place by acting on what you believe. You have to act on it, and you have to do it. That is why the Bible tells us, **But be doers of the word, and not hearers only...** (James 1:22).

Just believing is not going to change your circumstances. Let me show you this principle by the Scriptures.

Matthew 6:27-34:

> **Which of you by worrying can add one cubit to his stature?**

So why do you worry about clothing? Consider the lilies of the field, how they grow: they neither toil nor spin; and yet I say to you that even Solomon in all his glory was not arrayed like one of these.

Now if God so clothes the grass of the field, which today is, and tomorrow is thrown into the oven, will He not much more clothe you, O you of little faith?

Underline that word *faith.*

Therefore do not worry, saying, "What shall we eat?" or "What shall we drink?" or "What shall we wear?" For after all these things the Gentiles seek. For your heavenly Father knows that you need all these things.

But seek first the kingdom of God and His righteousness, and all these things shall be added to you.

Therefore do not worry about tomorrow, for tomorrow will worry about its own things. Sufficient for the day is its own trouble.

Notice the latter part of verse 30.

...O you of little faith....

Then notice verse 33:

But seek first the kingdom of God and His righteousness, and all these things shall be added to you.

3
Faith Requires Action

Now, if all faith means is basically believing something [going back to Mr. Strong's Greek definition: "persuasion, i.e., credence, moral conviction (of religious truth, or the truthfulness of God or a religious teacher), especially reliance upon Christ for salvation; abstractly [meaning] constancy in such profession; by extension the system of religious (Gospel) truth itself:—assurance, belief, believe, faith, fidelity"] then notice Matthew 6:30 again where it says *God so clothes the grass of the field.*

Now if God clothes the grass of the field, how does God get the grass *clothed*? Just by thinking about it? By believing? No! He has to actually overtly do something to get the grass clothed.

Your Faith Requires Action

Re-read verses 30-32, focusing on the first part of verse 32:

For after all these things the Gentiles seek....

"Seek." You cannot seek by sitting in a room believing something. Seeking is an overt action, not a thought. Can you agree with that? To seek, you would have to do something. Then Jesus caps it off with the thirty-third verse, saying...

But seek first the kingdom of God....

That is not just believing the Kingdom of God; that is doing something about the Kingdom of God. He said **seek** it.

21

...and His righteousness, and all these things shall be added to you.

Because if you seek the Kingdom first, you are going to find out how to get all the other things that the Gentiles are seeking after. And you will have to do something in order to get it. There is action implied in this faith, **O you of little faith** He said seek first the Kingdom. That is an active, overt act on our part. That is not sitting in a room believing the Kingdom exists. You have to seek it. You have to do something. That is an action. Faith is acting on what you believe.

Now I want to show that *action* is involved in each of the following Scriptures.

Matthew 8:5-10:

> **Now when Jesus had entered Capernaum, a centurion came to Him, pleading with Him, saying, "Lord, my servant is lying at home paralyzed, dreadfully tormented."**
>
> **And Jesus said to him, "I will come and heal him."**
>
> **The centurion answered and said, "Lord, I am not worthy that You should come under my roof. But only speak a word, and my servant will be healed. For I also am a man under authority, having soldiers under me. And I say to this one, 'Go,' and he goes; and to another, 'Come,' and he comes; and to my servant, 'Do this,' and he does it."**
>
> **When Jesus heard it, He marveled, and said to those who followed, "Assuredly, I say to you, I have not found such great faith, not even in Israel!"**

Authority Must Be Exercised

So the key words here are *great faith*. Jesus said *great faith*. Now notice how that faith was activated—by doing something, not by believing something. Because even if you have been given authority, you must still have action.

The centurion said, "I have generals over me"(maybe he was a colonel, captain or whatever), and I have privates under me. I tell one to go, and he goes. I tell another to come, and he comes." That is action.

Authority has to be exercised. You cannot sit in an office with authority and just think. You have to actually do something. You have to say something, do something, write something, or send something before any of your orders will be followed. That is *action*. It is not just believing something—you have to act.

If you have authority, you have to exercise it, or else the authority will not do you any good. This man recognized that with Jesus. He recognized that Jesus was a man of authority. Jesus said, **I will come and heal him.** The man said, "I am not worthy that You come. Just speak the Word, because Your Word spoken is the same as You coming.

"You do not have to come, just speak the Word. I am a man under authority, and I understand authority. Speak the Word and I know my servant will be healed. When I speak to one of my soldiers and I tell him to go, he goes. When I tell him to come, he comes. When I tell him to do something, he does" (author's paraphrase).

In great faith, action is involved. Jesus said, **I have not found such great faith, not even in Israel**. That great faith was demonstrated by what that man said about his authority to command someone to go and come and do.

So faith was activated by someone doing something, not just believing something. If the man had just believed that Jesus could do something and yet never came to Jesus and appealed to Him, his servant would not have been healed. And yet what he believed about Jesus would have been true, but it would not have affected his servant.

Are you following this? Then let us look at another passage of Scripture.

Matthew 8:23-26:

Now when He got into a boat, His disciples followed Him. And suddenly a great tempest arose on the sea, so that the boat was covered with the waves. But He was asleep. Then His disciples came to Him and awoke Him, saying, "Lord, save us! We are perishing!"

But He said to them, "Why are you fearful, O you of little faith?"

O you of little faith. Now if faith was just believing that the storm would stop and go away, that would be all they would have to do—just believe. Notice this last part of verse 26 carefully.

But He said to them, "Why are you fearful, O you of little faith?" *Then He arose and rebuked the winds and the sea, and there was a great calm.*

Notice that there was no calm until Jesus arose and did something. So when He talked to them about their faith, He was talking about an action. He said to them, **Why are you fearful, O you of little faith?** He was referring to an action—not just to believing something.

If all they had to do was believe and if all that faith meant was believe, then Jesus would not have had to get up from His nap. He could have just believed. The Bible says He *arose*. But He did not just arise and *look* at the storm, He arose and *did* something. He *rebuked* it. He did not just *rebuke*, He specifically rebuked the wind and the sea. He did both.

The Disciples Reacted in Fear

What was their little faith? That little faith was doing nothing except *reacting* to the circumstances instead of *responding* to the circumstances. *They reacted* in *fear. Jesus responded* in *faith.* Can you see that? He did not just believe that God was going to do something about the storm. In fact, God did *nothing* about the storm, Jesus did. He is the One Who did something. That Scripture says this: **He arose.** That is an action.

The reason He arose was because He believed if He did something about the storm and the sea, something would be done. So He did it—He arose and rebuked both the wind and the sea. Then the calm came. But the result was based upon an action. I wanted you to see that what Jesus did was an *action*. And He tied it in with faith. He said, **O you of little faith.** If things had been left in the disciples' hands, the boat would have sunk, because they were not responding—they were reacting.

I am demonstrating that faith is acting on what you believe, not just believing something.

Mark 2:1-12:

> **And again He entered Capernaum after some days, and it was heard that He was in the house. Immediately many gathered together, so that there was no longer room to receive them, not even near the door. And He preached the word to them.**
>
> **Then they came to Him, bringing a paralytic who was carried by four men. And when they could not come near Him because of the crowd, they uncovered the roof where He was. So when they had broken through, they let down the bed on which the paralytic was lying.**
>
> **When Jesus saw their faith...**[How in the world can you see faith? Faith is a principle. How can you see it?]**...He said to the paralytic, "Son, your sins are forgiven you."**
>
> **And some of the scribes were sitting there and reasoning in their hearts, "Why does this Man speak blasphemies like this? Who can forgive sins but God alone?"**
>
> **But immediately, when Jesus perceived in His spirit that they reasoned thus within themselves, He said to them, "Why do you reason about these things in your hearts? Which is easier, to say to the paralytic, 'Your sins are forgiven you,' or to say, 'Arise, take up your bed and walk'?**

"But that you may know that the Son of Man has power on earth to forgive sins"—He said to the paralytic, "I say to you, arise, take up your bed, and go to your house." Immediately he arose, took up the bed, and went out in the presence of them all, so that all were amazed and glorified God, saying, "We never saw anything like this!"

Look at verse 3 again, **Then they came to Him, bringing a paralytic who was carried by four men.** *They* is plural, so there had to be at least two people. It says, **Carried by four men.** So there were five people involved in this transaction: the four people who were carrying the man on the stretcher, and the man himself. When the four men carrying the paralytic arrived, they could not get in the house where Jesus was because of the crowd.

The Bible says that these four went up on top of the house, and began to lift up the roof tiles until they made a big enough hole through which they lowered the paralyzed man on the stretcher into the midst where Jesus was.

Those four men and the paralyzed man must have believed something or they would not have wasted their time bringing the sick man; and the paralyzed man would not have allowed them to take him on top of the roof. Can you imagine that scene? A paralyzed man on a stretcher being lifted up on a roof by four men. That paralyzed man *had* to be believing something.

Everything they believed was true, in that if they could get to Jesus this man could get delivered. That was true. But suppose they had never come. Then the man would not have been delivered. Then the assumption would have been made, "It is not God's will, because if it was His will, God would do something about it!" No! No! No!

Look at verse 3 again:

Then they came to Him, bringing....

Bringing implies action. Faith is acting on what you believe.

Look at verse 5 again: **When Jesus saw their faith....**

What did Jesus *see*? He saw four people up on top of the house tearing the roof off. He saw these four people wrap some ropes around the ends of the stretcher. He saw a paralyzed man on a stretcher and this man coming down through the roof into the room where He was. That is an action. They were not just believing something. They acted. And the Bible says Jesus called that "action" *faith*. *When Jesus saw their faith....* That is plural—that means the people who brought him and the man himself had to have faith.

I say to you, arise.... What a strange thing to say to someone who is paralyzed. Arise. Get up. Walk. Now if it had been like some people today, they would have said, "I don't know why this man is trying to embarrass me like this in front of all these people. Can't He see that I'm paralyzed? I can't walk. If I could have walked, I wouldn't have let these men lower me down through the ceiling of this house." That is the type of comment some people would have made.

PART II

HOW TO INCREASE
YOUR FAITH

4
Faith Requires Time To Grow

Matthew 9:20 (KJV):

> **And, behold, a woman, which was diseased with an issue of blood twelve years, came behind him, and touched the hem of his garment.**

Why on earth would this woman do something so stupid, to come and touch the hem of Jesus' garment? Notice it did not say she came and touched Him. She just touched His clothes. Now you know she had to have a revelation of that. Where did she get it? Probably by what she heard, because faith *comes* by hearing. She heard people talking about this man and the fact that if you could just touch His clothes, because He was so saturated with that healing power, you could get healed from it. Now let us notice the latter part of that 20th verse:

> **...and touched the hem of his garment.**

Then there is a *period*, and verse 21 says,

> **For she said....**

We do not usually use terms like *for* in this context. I like to substitute *because* whenever I see the word *for*. It flows much better in modern-day English. Now it would read like this:

Verse 20:

> **...and touched the hem of his garment.**

Verse 21:

> **For (Because)...**

That was the reason for doing it.

...she said within herself, if I may but touch his
garment, I shall be whole.

The Woman Had To Believe and Act

For her to touch His garment, she had to, number one,
believe it. But then she had to do it. What she believed was
true, but it would not have affected her if she had not done
it. Believing it did not change the situation. The change did
not come until she did what she believed.

Verse 22 (KJV):

**But Jesus turned him about, and when he saw her,
he said, Daughter, be of good comfort; thy faith hath
made thee whole. And the woman was made whole
from that hour.**

What was her faith? Her faith was to touch Him, which
was an action. She did not just sit on the side of the road
and believe. "Well, I believe if I can get close to Him I will
get healed." She did something. Are you following me? She
acted on what she believed. If you back up and look at the
story, the story says in verse 21:

**For she said within herself, If I may but touch his
garment, I shall be whole.**

That was absolutely true.

Now, because you have the complete story you know
from the story that was true. But you know what? It was
just as true before she touched Him, as it was after she
touched Him. It was not true *because* she touched Him. It
was true even before she touched Him. However, it was the
touching of Him based on what she believed that gave her,
personally, the benefit of what she believed. If she had just
believed it, it still would have been true, but it would not
have changed her circumstances. Can you see that?

This is so important to understand, and that is where
people are missing it. All over the world they are missing it,
and what is so tragic is that some of them will act like they

know it and do not want to receive any instruction, and I can see it in their lives. I see it because they do not have the results.

Faith Will Produce Results

Faith will produce results. *Over time*, faith will produce results, and so what happens, they get caught up in the euphoria of all of the expectations of what faith can produce and yet they still do not understand. They make an attempt to exercise faith. They do not see immediate results so they give up—but you have to stay with it.

It is like a marriage. You cannot judge the validity of a marriage on the first four or five years, and that is where many people lose the whole thing. It takes time to grow together. You are just getting to know the person after about five years—you are finally finding out how to spell their name. It takes time to learn one another. Many people throw up their hands, because they have a few encounters that are not pleasant. They figure that it is all over. "I don't love her anymore—she doesn't love me anymore." They don't give it time.

Marriage takes time. Anything of value takes time, and so it is with the principles of faith. It produces results over time. It is not an instant panacea for anything. It is not a rip cord that you pull to bail you out of some problem. It is not an Aladdin's lamp that you can stroke and say, "Genie, Genie, come out and give me a new yacht."

It does not work that way. You have to stay with it. You have to make a commitment. And you have to commit yourself to the point of burning all the bridges down behind you, and many of you have not done that. You are just trying faith as a gimmick. You want to see if it is going to work. Right there is doubt, and that is what has already crippled you. You have to be completely sold out. You have to be absolutely, unequivocally convinced.

You Have an Adversary

Remember, you have an adversary. You have an enemy, and he is going to stand in the road of your life and resist you every step of the way. You have to fight your way through (1 Timothy 6:12). You have to give it everything you have if you want to win. You have to stay with it until it produces results. Stay with it until it works. And in the process you will be criticized, falsely accused, and misunderstood, but *you* have to be convinced. I am absolutely, positively convinced.

I did not get convinced after walking in it for twenty-five years. I was convinced on the very first day I found out about it. That is why I have been with it for twenty-five years, and it has produced. But faith is an action. The woman said, "If I can but touch His clothes." That was true. Absolutely true. But it would not have done her any good *if* she had not touched. When she touched Him, power was released and Jesus called it faith. Jesus was the One Who said, **Daughter, *your* faith.** But what was her faith? Her faith was an action, it was not just believing something.

Start With Believing

Again, you have to start with the believing, because it is the believing that puts you into position to act, but if all you do is believe, even though what you believe is absolutely true, it will never change your circumstances.

Matthew 9:27,28:

> **When Jesus departed from there, two blind men followed Him...**

(What did they do? They did what? They followed Him. *Following* is an action, right?)

> **...crying out and saying, "Son of David, have mercy on us!"**

34

And when He had come into the house, the blind men came....

Came is an action.

...to Him. And Jesus *said* to them, "Do you believe that I am able to do this?"

"Lord, we do not know whether You can do anything or not, but it was such a hot day outside we figured that this would be a good opportunity for us to get in out of the sun. We do not know whether You can do anything or not. If You can, go ahead and do it, but we don't know." That is not what it says. No! No! Why did He ask them this question? He asked them this question to activate their faith. Notice the last part of verse 28:

They said to him "Yes, Lord."

Verses 29-31:

Then He touched their eyes, saying, "According to your faith let it be to you." And their eyes were opened. And Jesus sternly warned them, saying, "See that no one knows it." But when they had departed, they spread the news about Him in all that country.

Now go back to verse 29. It says:

Then He touched their eyes, saying, "According to your faith...."

It is interesting that He did not say *according to your believing*. He did not say to them, "Do you have faith for this?" He asked them the question, "Do you believe it?" They said, "Yes." Then He said, **According to your faith**...not "according to your belief." He asked them if they believed, but He did not say, "According to your believing," He said, "According to your faith."

What Was Their Faith?

Now what was their faith? Number one, their faith was the fact that they cried out to Him for mercy. And number two, they came. That was an action. If they had stayed outside, they would not have received. They acted on what they believed. They believed that if they could get to this Man Jesus, they could get some help.

Somehow they had heard about this Man, and they cried out for mercy, and then they acted—they came into the house, and then Jesus said to them, "Do you believe that I am able to do this?" And they said, "Yes, Lord." He said, "According to your faith." He did not say according to your believing, and yet, it was their believing that put *them* in position to act. Can you see that? So faith is acting on what you believe.

Peter Acted on His Belief

Matthew 14:25-29:

Now in the fourth watch of the night Jesus went to them, walking on the sea. And when the disciples saw Him walking on the sea, they were troubled, saying, "It is a ghost!" And they cried out for fear.

But immediately Jesus spoke to them, saying, "Be of good cheer! It is I; do not be afraid."

And Peter answered Him and said, "Lord, if it is You, command me to come to You on the water."

So He said, "Come." And when Peter had come down out of the boat....

So Peter acted, did he not? They did not push him out of the boat. It said,

And when Peter had come down out of the boat....

That leaves no doubt as to what was happening here. The brother got out of the boat.

That is an action. So he must have believed that what Jesus said was true—come and walk on the water. He did not just believe it, but he acted. Did he not? Now watch this:

And when Peter had come down out of the boat, he walked on the water....

Peter walked on the water. He is the only man other than Jesus that we have any record of who ever walked on the water. How did he walk on the water? He acted on what he believed. He believed that when Jesus said *come,* Jesus meant *come,* and that is what Jesus was doing, walking on the water. Peter was saying in essence, "Hey, Lord, if that's You, let me come and walk." And Jesus said, "Come." "Come" will require not just a belief, but an action.

And when Peter had come down out of the boat, he walked on the water to go to Jesus.

Verse 30:

But when he saw....

Saw has to do with the sense world. The sense realm.

...when he saw that the wind was boisterous, he was afraid....

The circumstances will always bring fear. If you look at the circumstances, they will bring fear. If you look at the Word of God, you will walk on the water. Now, we *do not* deny the circumstances. The wind was blowing. There was no question about it.

...when he saw that the wind was boisterous....

The word *boisterous* means strong and tempestuous. It was blowing. But wait a minute. It was blowing on Jesus, and He was walking. So what is the problem? If the Master was walking in the wind, and the Master said come, what are you afraid of?

But when he saw that the wind was boisterous, he was afraid; and beginning to sink....

If You Look at the Circumstances, You Will Sink

Perhaps that is where you have missed it. You started looking at the circumstances. When you look at the circumstances you will begin to sink. As long as you keep your eyes on the circumstances and off of the Word of God, you will sink. Multitudes of Christians are going down just because of that. You cannot look at the circumstances. I will say it again, you do not deny their existence, but you deny them the authority to dictate the terms of your life. That is a big difference. Yes, the wind was blowing, but Jesus was standing in the wind. Now watch this.

Verses 30,31:

...beginning to sink he cried out, saying, "Lord, save me!"

And immediately Jesus stretched out His hand and caught him, and said to him, "O you of little faith...."

Jesus did not say that Peter did not have any faith. I do not know if you can grasp the enormity of this revelation. He said,

O you of *little* faith.

Here is this man walking on water *with little faith*. What could he do *with great faith*? Probably fly. That goes to show you the potency of your faith. If you could walk on water with a little, what could you do with much faith? Let us read on:

...and caught him, and said to him, "O you of little faith, *why* did you doubt?"

Why did you doubt? You know why—because he took his eyes off of the Word of God and began to look at the circumstances. Every time you do it, you are going to go down. You are going to begin to sink. Your life is going to sink. Your marriage is going to sink. Your job, your business is going to sink. Your finances are going to sink. We do not deny what we see, we just deny its authority to tell us how to act and how to respond to the issues of life.

Jesus was walking on the same boisterous water, Jesus was standing in the same wind, and He did not go down.

He said, **"O you of little faith, why did you doubt?"** That is why it is important for you to know that you can have the Word of God, you can know the Word of God, you can have the will of God, you can know the will of God and still go down the tubes. Why did you doubt? Faith is acting on what you believe.

Now understand, even though you act on it, that action can still be affected by the circumstances *if you allow them to*. That is why Second Corinthians 4:18 says,

> **While we do not look at the things which are seen, but at the things which are not seen. For** (or because) **the things which are seen are temporary** (or subject to change), **but the things which are not seen are eternal.**

Paul said, **While we do not look at the things which are seen.** He did not say to deny their existence. He did not say they do not exist. He simply said, *do not look at them. Do not let them dictate the terms of your existence.* Let God's Word do that. What does God's Word say?

Philippians 4:19:

And my God shall supply all your need....

I do not care if they cut the welfare. I do not care if Social Security goes out of business. I do not want it to, but that has nothing to do with me making it in life. If you look at those things, they will scare your pants off. If you look at all the things that are going on around our nation and around our cities, it will scare you silly.

We do not deny the things, and we do what we can to affect them in a positive way. But I cannot let them dictate the terms of my existence, because they are not my source. *God is my source! God's Word is my source,* and *faith* is what *activates God's power.* But it is an action. I have to act on what I believe, and *what I believe ought to be based on what the Word of God says,* not on my little Mickey Mouse brain, trying to figure something out in the natural. There is a place for my brain and a place to use it at the right time, but when it comes to the things of God, if God tells me to walk, then I had better walk!

5

Faith Is Persistent

Now, let us go on to Matthew 15. Let me show you another Scripture that shows us without question that faith is action. It is acting on what you believe.

Matthew 15:21,22:

> Then Jesus went out from there and departed to the region of Tyre and Sidon. And behold, a woman of Canaan came from that region and cried out to Him, saying, "Have mercy on me, O Lord, Son of David! My daughter is severely demon-possessed."

The Woman Left Her Region

Why did you suppose this lady left her region and came to Him and cried, saying, **"...Have mercy on me, O Lord, Son of David!..."**? She probably heard about Jesus. So what? **So then faith *comes* by hearing, and hearing by the word of God** (Rom. 10:17). That is why she came and cried after Him. *She believed something.* She believed that *if* she *could* get to Him, her daughter could get some help. Undoubtedly, she believed that, or she never would have left her region to come and find Him. So, she believed something.

Verses 23-25:

> But He answered her not a word. And His disciples came and urged Him, saying, "Send her away, for she cries out after us."
>
> But He answered and said, "I was not sent except to the lost sheep of the house of Israel."

41

Then she came and worshiped Him, saying....

Verse 25 says, **Then she came....**

The Woman Kept Coming

She kept on coming. She kept on following. She acted on what she believed. She believed that she could get some help for her daughter so she did not stay in Canaan and believe that, because she never would have received any help. She did something about it. She acted on what she believed. She came. And even when the Lord said what *He* said, she came. How discouraging what He said had to be, *even though* He did not say that to discourage her, but to find out, "Do you really have faith? Do you really believe this or are you just blowing in the wind? Are you just talking to hear your gums rattle? Do you really believe it?"

He already knew what He was going to do. But this statement was designed to locate her for her own benefit. How much do you really want this? How much do you really believe that God can help you? *Came* is an *action*. Is that right? She did something. She did not just believe, she came!

Verses 25-28:

Then she came and worshiped Him, saying, "Lord, help me!" But He answered and said, "It is not good to take the children's bread and throw it to the little dogs." And she said, "Yes, Lord, yet even the little dogs eat the crumbs which fall from their masters' table."

Then Jesus answered and said to her, "O woman, great is your faith! Let it be to you as you desire." And her daughter was healed from that very hour.

Jesus called it faith. Did you notice that? He said, **...great is your faith.** What was her great faith? She left her own *region*, came—came, that is an action—and found Him. And then even after He said, **...I was not sent except**

42

to the lost sheep of the house of Israel, the woman did not stop. She did not give up. She pressed on. She stayed right there, and she got what she wanted because she persisted. She believed it. You know she believed it because she stayed with it.

That is where some people miss it. They will stand for five minutes if it is easy. But if they get any opposition, then they are ready for something new. They have not mastered the old yet, but they are ready for something new. She stayed with it. Everything she did was an action. She acted on what she believed. *Faith is acting*. If you do not act on it, it will never come to pass.

Matthew 16:5-12:

Now when His disciples had come to the other side, they had forgotten to take bread.

Then Jesus said to them, "Take heed and beware of the leaven of the Pharisees and the Sadducees."

And they reasoned among themselves, saying, "It is because we have taken no bread."

But Jesus, being aware of it, said to them, "O you of little faith, why do you reason among yourselves because you have brought no bread? Do you not yet understand, or remember the five loaves of the five thousand and how many baskets you took up? Nor the seven loaves of the four thousand and how many large baskets you took up? How is it you do not understand that I did not speak to you concerning bread?—*but* to beware of the leaven of the Pharisees and Sadducees." Then they understood that He did not tell them to beware of the leaven of bread, but of the doctrine of the Pharisees and Sadducees.

What is the point here? Watch it. Here is the clue, in verse 7:

And they reasoned among themselves, saying, "It is because we have taken no bread."

In other words, they had brought no bread with them. Bringing bread would have been an action, would it not? It would not have been a belief, it would have been an action. Verses 7 and 8 again:

> And they reasoned among themselves, saying, "It is because we have taken no bread."

> But Jesus, being aware of it, said to them, "O you of little faith...."

Jesus Tied Their Faith To Their Action

Notice how He puts the faith together with the fact that they had not brought any bread. In other words, there was no action. That is what they thought, because they thought He was talking about bread to eat. He was not. He was talking about the doctrine of the religious leaders, but it still demonstrates action because He said, ..."O you of little faith."

What was the little faith? To not bring any bread, if in fact, He had been talking about actual physical bread. If He were talking about actual physical bread, and they had brought the bread, the bringing of the bread would have been an action, would it not?

Matthew 17:14-16:

> And when they had come to the multitude, a man came to Him, kneeling down to Him and saying, "Lord, have mercy on my son, for he is an epileptic and suffers severely; for he often falls into the fire and often into the water. So I brought him to Your disciples....

Now wait a minute. ...**So I brought him**. Is that an action? He must have brought his son because he believed that the disciples could do something to help his son; otherwise, he would not have brought his son. That is an action.

Verses 16-20:

"So I brought him to Your disciples, but they could not cure him."

Then Jesus answered and said, "O faithless and perverse generation, how long shall I be with you? How long shall I bear with you? Bring him here to Me." And Jesus rebuked the demon, and it came out of him; and the child was cured from that very hour.

Then the disciples came to Jesus privately and said, "Why could we not cast it out?"

So Jesus said to them, "Because of your unbelief; for assuredly, I say to you, if you have faith as a mustard seed, you will say to this mountain, 'Move from here to there,' and it will move; and nothing will be impossible for you."

Now, verse 21 says,

"However, this kind does not go out except by prayer and fasting."

Notice verse 19 again.

Then the disciples came to Jesus privately and said, "Why could we not cast it out?"

That is a question. Can you agree with that?

Verse 20:

So Jesus said to them, "Because of your unbelief...."

That is the answer, is it not? That is the answer to their question, period! Now, where is the action part here? Well, the action is the fact, number one, the man brought his child, and number two, the disciples did not do anything. They failed to act, but Jesus did act.

...And Jesus rebuked the demon....

That is an action, because Jesus believed that when He rebuked the demon, the demon would go. So, He did it. So, faith was an action. Now, here is another great and powerful truth, verse 19:

Then the disciples came to Jesus *privately* and said, "Why could we not cast it out?"

They asked a question. In other words, in modern English, "Why could we not do it?" I want you to get this truth, so let me demonstrate. I want this truth to really hit you, because this is so important, and can be such a blessing to you. Now, watch this object lesson. I go to my family doctor and say, "Dr. Jones, I have a real serious problem. My mind is giving me some real challenges. I do not understand why I cannot get pregnant."

Would that be a stupid question for me, as a male, to ask a doctor? Yes! Why? Because males cannot get pregnant. Here is my point. The very fact that the disciples asked Jesus why they could not cast the demon out means that *they could* have cast it out, because if they could not have cast it out, they would have known they could not, and would not have asked a stupid question like, "How come I cannot get pregnant?" The very fact that they asked why they could not meant that they knew that they could, but for some reason *this time,* it did not work.

The Disciples Had the Authority

If they knew that they could not do it, they would have known that it was because they did not have the ability or the authority. But, they had the authority, because in the tenth chapter of Matthew, verse 1, Jesus *gave them that authority*. They knew they could do it. They had the authority, they had the ability, but for some reason, this time it did work. So they said, "Why could we not cast it out?" Jesus did not say, "Because you did not have the ability or the authority," He said, **Because of your unbelief.** So, that means that if they had believed it and acted on it, they could have cast the demon out.

It is also obvious from the fact that Jesus cast out the demon that it was the will of God for the demon to go. But you see, in our time, we would have said, "Well, Reverend so-and-so did not cast the demon out, so that means it was not God's will, because if it was God's will, the demon would have gone." Not if you are not operating in faith. Maybe you had the wrong person praying for you.

It Is God's Will To Cast Out Demons

"Well, I went to another church and it did not work." Maybe you went to the wrong church. We never think that it could be us. *Not my fault!* "The erudite and scholarly Dr. Frederick K. C. Price, Ph.D.—it could not be me. It has to be that it is not the will of God." We think, "Well, it did not work, so it must not be God's will."

Verses 20,21:

If you have faith as a mustard seed, you will say to this mountain, "Move from here to there," and it will move; and nothing will be impossible for you. However, this kind does not go out except by prayer and fasting.

Fasting Does Not Cast Out Demons

Now, I do not want to get into an argument or debate with people about the statement, ...**However, this kind does not go out except by prayer and fasting,** because they do not know and I do not know. It does not seem to fit in this situation, because if you stop and think about it, if it is fasting that casts out demons, just praying and fasting, then the Hindus ought to be able to cast out more demons than any Christian ever thought about casting out. Their whole life is a life of fasting to the point of skin and bones.

So if fasting is going to do it, then that would be a work of the flesh anyway. The demon would be going out on the basis of some work you performed by fasting and denying your flesh. Then, you would have to have a chart or list of all the different kinds of demons, and you would have to know how many fast days you have to put in to cast out that kind of demon; besides that, people cannot even miss one meal, let alone go one day without eating. The demon could end up killing the person while you are trying to fast two days.

If there is a demon that only goes out after a forty-day fast, and you cannot go forty minutes without eating something, how are you going to get the demon cast out? Demons are cast out by His Word. There are other Scriptures where it says that He cast out the spirits with His Word, not with His fasting. If you read the four gospels, you will find out about many kinds of demons. There are unclean spirits, blind spirits, deaf and dumb spirits.

Some people Jesus ministered to could not talk or hear, but when the spirit was cast out, their tongue was loosed. So, how many days do you fast for a deaf and dumb spirit? If the statement was or was not in the original, I cannot say. One thing for sure, Jesus' answer to their question is consistent with Biblical principle when he said, **Because of your unbelief**, meaning their failure to act in faith. They had the authority.

Here is another very important lesson. Even when you have the authority of God, if you do not exercise faith, it is still not going to work for you. Authority has to be exercised. A police officer can be given the authority to arrest or apprehend criminals. He can stand right in front of a store, see a criminal go in, rob the store, walk out of the store and right up in front of him, look him in the eye and say, "Boo!" That criminal can jump in his car and drive away if the police officer does not exercise his authority. Just because he has the authority does not arrest the criminal.

Let us look at another Scripture.

Matthew 21:21:

> So Jesus answered and said to them, "Assuredly, I say to you, if you have faith and do not doubt, you will

not only do what was done to the fig tree, but also if you say to this mountain, 'Be removed and be cast into the sea,' it will be done."

He said, "Not only do." That is an action. *Do* is an *action*.

...do what was done to the fig tree....

Saying Is Action

He had cursed the tree. So, He was saying to them, "Not only this that had been done to the fig tree, but also, if you say...if you say." That is not believing something; that is doing something. **If you say**—that is an action. A verbal action. You have to do something. He did not say, "If you shall believe that the mountain will move, it will move." He said, **if you say to this mountain...it will be done**.

Now here is what you do when you read that. You are thinking in your mind of walking up to a mountain and saying, "Move! In Jesus' name, I command you to move." Not necessarily. I want the mountain moved. It does not matter how, I just want it moved. God does not have to supernaturally move the mountain, if I have the wherewithal to move the mountain.

Engineers are moving mountains on a daily basis. They can take a whole mountain down. Do you know how they move the mountain? Someone speaks to it, and then someone speaks to other people and says, "Move that mountain," and the mountain gets moved. See, in your mind you get the idea you are going to see a physical mountain jump up and move. Now, I am not saying that cannot occur, but it does not have to if you have the capability of moving that mountain. Someone still has to believe it and speak to it.

6

Faith Is Acting on What You Believe

Now in all these Scriptures, this revelation is here, *that faith is acting on what you believe.* I have been reading this for twenty-five years, and I did not see this revelation until recently when the Spirit of God pointed this out. He said, "Fred, here is your confirmation for the principle that you have been teaching for twenty-five years." I knew the principle was right, but I was not aware of putting it together with all these different references to substantiate that what I have been saying for twenty-five years is absolutely true, that *faith is an action.*

Matthew 23:23, Jesus is speaking:

> **Woe to you, scribes and Pharisees, hypocrites! For you pay tithe of mint and anise and cummin....**

Underline the word *pay.* Is *pay* a belief or an action? You cannot get that credit card payment satisfied by believing, can you? *Hallelujah*! You cannot get that credit card bill in the mail, open the envelope, and say, "I believe it is paid. Hallelujah!" You better send those folks some money. "Pay," is an action, not just a belief. Right? Notice again:

> **Woe to you, scribes and Pharisees, hypocrites! For you pay tithe of mint and anise and cummin, and have neglected the weightier matters of the law: justice....**

Justice is something that has to be exercised. You cannot just believe justice into being. You have to do something to demonstrate justice. Justice is an action.

Mercy Must Be Demonstrated

Another example is *mercy*. You cannot just believe mercy into existence. Mercy has to be demonstrated. How? By action. I owe someone $25,000, and he tells me, "If you don't pay me my money by sundown, I am going to have you put in jail," and I fall down in front of him and say, "Oh, no, Sir, have mercy on me. Have mercy on me."

"No, I am going to put you in jail, Dr. Price. I want my money." "Oh, please, please, Sir, my little boy and my wife—they are going to be lost without me if I go to jail." And I finally get through to the man, and he has mercy. He says, "I forgive the debt." That is an action, right? Mercy has to be demonstrated in some way. It is an action. Verse 23 again:

> ...and mercy and faith....

So *faith* has to be an *action* just like *mercy* and just like *justice*. Now notice this:

> ...These you ought to have (believed?)....

No!

> ...These you ought to have done....

That is an action, right? Let us go on.

We are still talking about an action. We are not through yet.

Mark 10:46-50:

> **Now they came to Jericho. As He went out of Jericho with His disciples and a great multitude, blind Bartimaeus, the son of Timaeus, sat by the road begging.**
>
> **And when he heard....**

Glory to God. What happens when you hear? *Faith comes by hearing, and hearing by the word of God* (Rom. 10:17).

And when he heard that it was Jesus of Nazareth, he began to (believe in his heart that Jesus of Nazareth could give him his eyesight).

Not so.

And when he heard that it was Jesus of Nazareth, he began to cry out....

That is an action. He did not just sit there and believe something, *he acted!* He cried out.

...he began to cry out and say, "Jesus, Son of David, have mercy on me!"

Then many warned him to be quiet; but he cried out all the more, "Son of David, have mercy on me!"

He was acting.

Verse 49:

So Jesus stood still and commanded him to be called. Then they called the blind man, saying to him, "Be of good cheer...."

Now, these rascals, a moment ago, were telling him to shut up. That is the same group that says, "Hosanna," and a few hours later, "Crucify Him." You better listen to God and not man, because man will mess you up royally.

"...Be of good cheer, Rise, He is calling you."

And (sitting steadfastly in his spot, continued to believe with all that was in him that the Son of God could have mercy upon him and heal his blindness).

It does not say that, does it? No!

And throwing aside his garment, he rose and came to Jesus.

The Blind Man Was Doing Something

Do you think he was just believing something? No, he was doing something. Number one, *casting away his garment.* Number two, he *rose.* That is an action. You cannot rise sitting down. Number three, he *came.* I love it. *Casting away, rose,* and *came,* all actions based on the belief that the Son of God could do him some good. But, if he had just believed it, he would not have received anything.

Verses 51,52:

So Jesus answered and said to him, "What do you want Me to do for you?" The blind man said to Him, "Rabboni, that I may receive my sight."

Then Jesus said to him, "Go your way; *your faith....*

Your what?

...your faith has....

What?

...Your faith has made you....

Wait a minute. Faith! Where was faith? Where was the action? What did he do? *Cried out, cast his garment away, rose and came.*

All *actions.* Hallelujah!

Jesus Called Action Faith

Notice, this is the Master speaking. Jesus called it faith. He did not call it believing. He called it faith. Cried out, cast his garment away, rose and came. Everyone of those are actions. Jesus did not say, "Your believing has made you whole." He said, "Your faith did it."

Then Jesus said to him, "Go your way; your faith...."

Remember now, he cried out, cast off his garment, rose, and came. All actions. Notice this (here is the revelation for you)....

Then Jesus said to him, **Go your way; your faith** (*is making* **you well**).

...**Go your way; your faith** (*will make* **you well**).

No!

...your faith *has*....

It is a done deal.

...your faith has made you well.

Is that the end of the story? No! It says,

And immediately he received....

That is an action.

...his sight....

Jesus did not touch him. Jesus did not cast out a blind spirit. The man received, but he could not receive until the power was available and the power was not available until he cried out, cast off his garment, rose, and came. He received. But now wait a minute, before he ever received, Jesus said, "Your faith *has*. He did not say *it is making* you well, present tense. It is already done.

It Takes Faith To Receive From God

But he still had to do something—he received his sight. Many of you cry, cast off your garment, rise, and come. Then when you get to Him and He says, "What do you need? What do you want?" You say, "I need to be healed. I need my needs met. I need finances. I need a job. I need something."

Then He says to you, "Your faith has made you well." And instead of receiving it, you go to crying some more. "Lord, have mercy on me. Oh, Jesus, oh Jesus, help me, Master. Oh, Lord help me." *No! No!* The man received. You do it by *faith*.

The power is present. The need is met. You have to believe it and then begin to say it. "*I believe I am healed. I believe I have a job. I believed I have whatever it is I need.*" And then you have to begin to see yourself with it, and once you see yourself with it, then stop crying, begging, and complaining. Then that is when it will manifest. But *you have to stay with it.*

This is where the fight of faith comes in, because Satan is going to rush in like a flood, to try to discourage you, to intimidate you, to tell you, "You do not see any change, do you? You do not feel any better, do you? You do not see any more money, do you?" You have to say, "I do not care what I see, I do not care what I feel, I have it because God said it. Amen!" That is how it works.

The FaithDome Was Built by Faith

That is how we got the FaithDome. While some were sleeping, while some got tired of the battle, while some gave up on it, for three years, I kept saying it. Every day. I would never give up. Every morning when my eyes would open, I said, "Father, I thank You. I believe the FaithDome is built. I believe that we have all the money. I believe that it is done. I believe that we have it," and then every time I would walk onto the grounds of Crenshaw Christian Center, I would look down to that empty spot of ground and I would see, by faith, the Dome standing there. I would see it in my spirit.

The devil would say, "You'll never get it done." Preachers were saying (when they should have been encouraging me, when they should have been getting behind me and saying, "Go for it, Fred. Stay with it, Fred. Keep on trucking, Fred"), "He will never get it built. They will never build that FaithDome."

I have news for you. *It is done!* We are in it. Glory to God! Not only are we in it, but it is paid for. I stayed on it, I never gave up. I said, "I *never gave up!*" I *cried* and I *cast off* my garment, I *rose* and I *came*. Glory to God! Amen!

God wants to do the same thing for you, but you have to be willing to burn all the bridges down. You have to be willing to take the criticism. You have to be willing to stand on God's unchanging Word. I do not care if it takes twenty-five million years, you have to be willing to stand. You have to be prepared to stand. You have to be willing to take all of the flack, all of the criticism, all of the misunderstanding, and stand right there.

That is what we have been doing, my wife and I, for twenty-five years, and we are going to stand for another twenty-five more after that, and we are going to keep on receiving everything that God said belongs to us. Instead of you getting jealous about me driving a Rolls Royce, instead of you getting jealous about me wearing nice clothes, instead of you getting jealous about me wearing a diamond ring, instead of you getting jealous about me living in a good house, *get yourself together and believe God.* Glory to God, *it works*! God wants you to have it all. Jesus said it Himself.

John 10:10:

I have come that they may have life, and that they may have it more abundantly.

And I am a living example of it. That is why I talk about it—not brag about it—but to let you know it is there. It is available. It is there, but you are going to have to be willing to stand, and having done all, stand! (Eph. 6:13.) Stand therefore. I never get tired of winning. I never get tired of hitting home runs. I do not know what the bases look like, because I do not stop on bases. Glory to God, and I am swinging for the fence. A grand slam every time. There it goes—going, going, going, gone! Amen.

It works. It is an action. Faith is *acting* on what you believe. You say you believe the Word of God, then act on it. Talk the Word, do not talk the circumstances. Talk the solution—not the problem. That is what causes it to work. You have to be willing and committed to take a stand. It is for *life*. You cannot say, "Well, I am going to try this." You have already lost. You cannot try it. You have to *do it*! You cannot find *trying* in the New Testament. There is no word *try*. It is only *do*!

7

How To Activate Faith

Luke 7:36-50:

> Then one of the Pharisees asked Him to eat with him. And He went to the Pharisee's house, and sat down to eat. And behold, a woman in the city who was a sinner, when she knew that Jesus sat at the table in the Pharisee's house, brought....

Underline the word brought. *Brought*. That is an *action*, right?

> ...brought an alabaster flask of fragrant oil, and stood....

She did not sit, she *stood*. That is an action, is it not?

> ...at His feet behind Him weeping....

That is an *action*, right? *Weeping* is an *action*.

> ...and she began to wash His feet....

That is an action. *Washing feet* is an *action*.

> ...with her tears, and wiped them....

That is an action.

> ...with the hair of her head; and she kissed His feet....

That is an action.

> ....and anointed them with the fragrant oil.

That is an action.

Now when the Pharisee who had invited Him saw this, he spoke to himself, saying, "This Man, if He were a prophet, would know who and what manner of woman this is who is touching Him...."

Even the Pharisee perceived action. Touching is an *action.*

"...for she is a sinner."

And Jesus answered and said to him, "Simon, I have something to say to you."

So he said, "Teacher, say it."

"There was a certain creditor who had two debtors. One owed five hundred denarii, and the other fifty.

"And when they had nothing with which to repay, he freely forgave them both. Tell Me, therefore, which of them will love him more?"

Simon answered and said, "I suppose the one whom he forgave more."

And He said to him, "You have rightly judged."

Then He turned to the woman and said to Simon, "Do you see this woman? I entered your house; you gave Me no water for My feet, but she has washed My feet with her tears and wiped them with the hair of her head. You gave Me no kiss, but this woman has not ceased to kiss My feet since the time I came in. You did not anoint My head with oil, but this woman has anointed My feet with fragrant oil. Therefore I say to you, her sins, which are many, are forgiven, for she loved much. But to whom little is forgiven, the same loves little."

Then He said to her, "Your sins are forgiven."

And those who sat at the table with Him began to say to themselves, "Who is this who even forgives sins?"

Then He said to the woman, "Your faith...."

Your what? *Your faith!*

"...has saved you. Go in peace."

Jesus called her weeping, *faith*. Jesus called her standing, *faith*. Jesus called what she brought, *faith*. Jesus called her anointing his feet, *faith*. Jesus called her wiping the tears with her hair, *faith*. All of these are *actions*. Is that right? Jesus called it *faith*. The *woman did something*. She *acted*. Jesus called it *faith*. Can you see that?

Luke 17:5,6:

> **And the apostles said to the Lord, "*Increase* our faith."**

So it must be possible to increase faith. It can get bigger. It can grow.

> **So the Lord said, "If you have faith as a mustard seed, you can say...."**

You can *say*, not you can believe.

> **"...to this mulberry tree, 'Be pulled up by the roots and be planted in the sea,' and it would obey you"** (provided you say something to it).

Saying Is an Action

Saying is an *action*. You have to act on what you believe. He said, "You can say." Understand, there are two ways to release your faith. First of all, it is by what you say, and then by an action that is commensurate with what you have said. So Jesus said, "You shall say."

That is how faith is activated: *by the words of our mouth, by saying it*! You cannot just believe it—you have to say it. "Yeah, but if I say something and it does not come to pass; what is it going to look like?" Do not be concerned about it—you have already missed it. If you have a reservation about saying it, then you will never activate your faith. You have to say it.

They said, **increase our faith**. They did not ask Him how to get faith. They did not ask Him, "Where can we go and find some?" They said *increase* it. Jesus gave them the secret to increasing it, and that is by *talking it* or *saying it*.

Here is a good example for you. I am always talking about the things of God, and what happens is, you get criticized when you talk the Word of God. When people do not understand, they will call you a braggart. They will say that you are arrogant. They will say you are self-centered. They will even say that you are materialistic, but they do not realize I am doing exactly what Jesus said.

I want my faith to increase, and He said, "You can *say*." *You* means *me*. He said, "You have to say it." I have been saying it for twenty-five years, and my faith has been getting stronger and stronger. And while the critics are criticizing, my faith is ever increasing. You have to talk about it, and you have to say it out loud so that the devil can hear it, because he is the one who is holding back your blessing, not God.

You cannot just have a thought in your mind. You have to *say* it. You cannot be ashamed, and you cannot be intimidated by what people are going to say, because they are going to say what they want to say if you do not say anything. So, you might as well say something that is going to help you.

I have been talking this talk, and I have been walking this walk for twenty-five years, and I have the goods to prove that it works. They said, **increase our faith**. Jesus did not say, "Run down to the gym and do twenty-five push-ups, jog three miles three times a week." No, He said:

If you have faith as a mustard seed, you can say....

He did not say you can think. He said, *say*.

...to this mulberry tree, "Be pulled up by the roots and be planted in the sea," and it would obey you.

You Must Believe When You Say

You have to really believe that in order to say it, because right away you could be intimidated by your friends and relatives. "Well, what are they going to say? They are going to think I am crazy." They already think you are crazy if you go to church more than once a week. Anyone who goes to church more than once a week has got to be out of their mind. Something is wrong with their head. They are fanatical. "You better be careful, if you get too much church it is going to affect your brain. They are going to put you in the nut house."

Now, it is not fanaticism if you go to a stadium that is open and exposed to the weather with 100,000 screaming, beer-drinking fans sitting around you, and the clouds come up and the rain, and the snow starts falling and twenty-two college graduates are chasing a pig full of air up and down the field.

Now that is not fanaticism. That is intelligent. If you do that, that is not fanaticism, that is sports. You are a fan, not a fanatic, and you do not have any problem saying to your friends, "I am going to the game." *Saying* is an action. Jesus said, "You can say."

The Ten Lepers Had To Believe Jesus

While we are in this same seventeenth chapter, let's look at verses 11 and 12:

> Now it happened as He went to Jerusalem that He passed through the midst of Samaria and Galilee. Then as He entered a certain village, there met Him ten men who were lepers, who stood afar off.

Leprosy was a disease that required, by the law of Moses, that if a person contracted it, he had to live apart from the mainstream of society. Lepers were treated as outcasts and had to live in colonies by themselves.

One of the requirements was that if they ever left the leper colony on the way somewhere and saw someone on the road ahead of them coming towards them, they would have to cry out, "Unclean, unclean," and that would alert the people approaching that this was a leper and they would want to avoid them. That is why they stood afar off.

Verse 13:

And they lifted up their voices and said, "Jesus, Master, have mercy on us!"

So, they must have recognized Who He was. They must have heard about Who He was, and about Him extending mercy to people. They took a big chance by saying, "Have mercy on us," instead of crying out "Unclean, unclean." Now, they had enough sense to stay their distance, but they cried out and said, "Lord, have mercy." Now notice this:

Verse 14:

So when He saw them, He said to them, "Go, show yourselves to the priests."

Now, the law of Moses required that if a person was a leper, as I previously stated, they had to live apart in a colony by themselves. However, if the leper was recovered, if the leprosy left the person, they were required under the law of Moses to go to the priests to be examined. Based upon a certain formula or procedure that the priests would go through, the priest would certify that the person had been cleansed of the leprosy. Then, an announcement, as it were, would be made and the individual would be clear to be reintroduced into the mainstream of society.

Now, watch the wisdom of God, and the mercy of God. You did not go to the high priest until *after* the leprosy was gone—not before the fact, but after the fact. If you can see this, this is rich. You see, when Jesus said, **Go, show yourselves to the priests,** in the mind of God, those ten men were already cleansed. Why? Because God calls those things which do not exist as though they did, and it is calling those things which do not exist as though they did, that causes them to come to be. Now watch this.

> **"Go, show yourselves to the priests." And so it was that as they went....**

That is an action.

> **...they were cleansed.**

As they *went*. In other words, while they were acting, that is when the manifestation came. Your natural desire is to wait until you see it. Then you will believe it, then you will accept it, then you will talk about it. But I have news for you—it will *never come to pass*. "As they *went*."

As far as God was concerned, they were already healed. That is why He told them to **Go, show**. But you see, they had to believe that and do that. It was not enough for them to just believe it. They had to do it!

I can imagine one of them saying, "Man, I don't know about you, George, but I ain't going to let this guy make a fool out of me. Don't you know what's going to happen? Look at you. You're just as leprous as you can be, and He's telling us to go show ourselves to the priest.

"I don't know why Jesus is trying to embarrass us like this. I mean, doesn't He know that if we go to the priest and we still have this leprosy, the priest is going to turn us around and tell us to come right back to the colony? Well, I tell you what, He ain't going to make no fool out of me."

The other guy said, "Wait a minute, man. Wait! Wait! Don't be so quick to act like that. We're the ones who cried out. He didn't cry out. He was minding His own business. We're the ones who said, 'Have mercy,' and He told us what to do. He said, **Go, show yourselves to the priests**."

"Yeah, but man, we're still lepers."

"I don't understand it, my brother, but the Man told us to go to the priests. I'm a leper now, I can't be any more than a leper after I go to the priests. Worst case scenario, I'll be what I was, because I'm already what I am. So, it doesn't make any difference. I have nothing to lose, only something to gain. So, I might as well go ahead and go to the priests."

And so the Bible says that as they went, they were cleansed. That is when the manifestation came, while they were *acting*, not believing—but they had to believe Jesus in order to, (*as they went*), act.

Verses 15-19:

And one of them, when he saw that he was healed, returned, and with a loud voice glorified God, and fell down on *his* face at His (or Jesus') feet, giving Him thanks. And he was a Samaritan.

Now, watch this, here is a revelation.

So Jesus answered and said, "Were there not ten cleansed?"

That is a hundred percent. There were only ten of them and Jesus said, *were*. Watch it. He did not say *are* there, He said, "*Were*."

You see, when He said, **Go, show yourselves to the priests**, as far as Almighty God was concerned, it was forever settled in heaven, they were cleansed, and they believed it and acted on it.

Oh, if I could just get you to do that. You have to act on it before you ever see anything. You have to act on it before you ever understand anything. You have to act on it before you ever feel anything. If you believe it, then do it. Then as you *go, (act) on the Word, the manifestation will come.*

So Jesus answered and said, "Were there not ten cleansed? But where *are* the nine?

"Were there not any found who returned to give glory to God except this foreigner?"

Watch this now.

> **And He said to him, "Arise, go your way. Your faith....**

Your what?

> **...your faith....**

It wasn't God's power that made them well, and yet we know it was God's power, but it was *their faith that activated God's power*. He said, "Go your way."

> **...has made you well."**

And what was his faith? *He went! Action.* He did not just believe something. "Well, I believe if I go to the priests and show myself to the priests, I'll be healed." No!

Can you see the difference here? Now they had to believe that what Jesus said was true, but they had to also act on it. If they had not acted on it, it would not have done them any good. They did what they believed. He said, "*Go.*" They believed it.

It is obvious that they believed it, because they what? *Went!* So, Dear Reader, you say you believe God? "Oh, yes. Hallelujah." Well then, you need to do what the Man said. You believe God, *then do it!* That is the only way it is going to come into manifestation for you.

Luke 18:1:

> **Then He spoke a parable to them, that men always ought to pray and not lose heart.**

What do you do when you pray? *Say.* You do not pray if you do not say. If you did not say, you did not pray. All you did was thought, and God does not respond to thought. He responds to prayer. And there is no such animal as a non-verbal prayer. When the disciples came to Jesus and said, Luke 11:1, **Lord, teach us to pray**, He said, Luke 11:2, **"When you pray, say...."** He did not say, when you pray, "*think.*" He said, "*say.*"

Luke 18:1-5:

Then He spoke a parable to them, that men always ought to pray and not lose heart, saying: "There was in a certain city a judge who did not fear God nor regard man. Now there was a widow in that city; and she came to him, saying, 'Get justice for me from my adversary.' And he would not for a while; but afterward he said within himself, 'Though I do not fear God nor regard man, yet because this widow troubles me I will avenge her, lest by her continual coming she weary me.'"

Now, I am not teaching on this particular parable, but I want to extract a principle from it. It is a parable of action. That is what I want you to see. The judge said, **...lest by her continual coming** (coming is an action) **she weary me**.

Verses 6-8:

Then the Lord said, "Hear what the unjust judge said."

Now, watch this.

And shall God not avenge His own elect who cry out day and night to Him....

Crying or *praying* or *petitioning* God is an *action*, is it not?

...though He bears long with them? I tell you that He will avenge them speedily. Nevertheless, when the Son of Man comes, will He really find faith on the earth?"

Now, if you notice, you will find a question mark at the end of that eighth verse as though it were a question. It is not a question. He was not asking a question. He knows what He is going to find when He comes to the earth.

It started out by telling us, **Then He spoke a parable to them....** Then He illustrated by a word picture, but the bottom line of the word picture was someone coming—*coming*—and asking, *asking. Action*, in other words. That is the point. He said, **"...when the Son of Man comes, will He really find faith on the earth?"**

There Will Be Faith When Jesus Returns

That is not a question. It is a statement that is designed to arrest our attention. If faith will be here when He comes back, there will be people praying, and if there are people praying, there has to be faith, because you cannot pray without faith. It was designed to locate us.

For example, the Garden of Eden. The Bible says that Adam and Eve heard the sound of the Lord God walking in the garden in the cool of the day. This was after Adam had disobeyed. He and Eve, because of their disobedience— their sin—hid from God.

I believe that God used to come into the garden, in some form that Adam and Eve could actually see; if not, how are you going to hide from something you cannot see? How do you know that the place where you are hiding is not where the person is? God is a Spirit. You cannot see God. Well, how do I know that the place I am running to and hiding in is not where God is, if I cannot see Him?

So, they had to be able to see something to know to hide from it.

It says they heard the sound of the Lord God walking in the garden in the cool of the day. And they hid themselves. One of the attributes of God is omniscience, which means all knowing. When the sound of the Lord God came walking in the garden in the cool of the day, Adam hid himself. Then the Lord God called to Adam and said, "Adam, where are you?" Wait a minute! I thought God was omniscient, I thought God was omnipotent. I thought God was omnipresent, everywhere at the same time. Why would He have to ask a stupid question like, "Where are you, Adam?" No! No!

That was the same thing as this story here in Luke 18, ...When the Son of Man comes, will He really find faith on the earth? It is not a question. And when He said,

"...Adam...where are you?" it was not really a question. He knew right where Adam was. He was trying to get Adam's attention so that Adam would be cognizant or recognize the enormity of his mess-up.

It is kind of like Mama and Johnny. You are out there on the back porch ironing or wherever you do your ironing, maybe in a special utility room. Johnny comes in from school and you hear the door open. "Johnny, is that you?" "Yes, Mom." "Well, it won't be long before dinner. You can go out and play for a while, but I'll call you in about ten minutes for dinner."

And then a little bit later (that ironing room where you are ironing is close to the kitchen) you hear a noise. Clink, clink, clink. Now, that sound is a ceramic sound, and it is made when the ceramic lid of a ceramic cookie jar is being disturbed, and you know what that rascal is doing. He is into those chocolate chip cookies.

So you never even stop ironing, but you say loudly, "Johnny, what are you doing?" You know exactly what he is doing. You are not asking a question; you are saying that to arrest that little fellow's attention so that he does not get in trouble when Dad comes home, by eating those cookies and getting full on them and not eating dinner. Can you see that?

So, Jesus said, **When the Son of Man comes, will He really find faith?** Absolutely! He will find faith. He knows He is going to find faith because people will be praying, and it takes faith to pray, and *praying* is an *action*.

Luke 22:31,32:
And the Lord said, "Simon, Simon! Indeed, Satan has asked for you, that he may sift you as wheat. But I have prayed for you, that your faith should not fail; and when you have returned to Me, strengthen your brethren."

Faith Without Action Will Fail

He said, **But I have prayed for you, that your faith should not fail**. How can faith fail? It can fail to act. That is the only way it can fail, by not acting. *Faith is acting* on what you believe. Now, I have one last witness that I want to give you, from James 2. I want you to follow this carefully. Remember, we are illustrating the fact that faith is what?— *acting* on what you believe. Or, for the child of God, faith is acting on the Word of God.

James 2:14-18:

What does it profit, my brethren, if someone says he has faith but does not have works? Can faith save him? If a brother or sister is naked and destitute of daily food, and one of you says to them, "Depart in peace, be warmed and filled," but you do not give them the things which are needed for the body, what does it profit? Thus also faith by itself, if it does not have works, is dead.

But someone will say, "You have faith, and I have works." Show me your faith without your works, and I will show you my faith by my works.

When people get on my case about me talking about prosperity—about possessing things—they need to be cool, because what they do not know in their ignorance is that I am in line with the Word of God. I am covered by the Word of God.

Verse 18 again:

But someone will say, "You have faith, and I have works." Show me your faith without your works, and I will show you my faith by my works.

The FaithDome is a work that shows my faith. My Rolls Royce is a work that shows my faith. Instead of people criticizing me, they should be saying, "Well, praise God, I can see that faith works." I am just doing what the Bible says. Some people call me a braggart. I am not bragging, I am doing exactly what the Bible says. Verse 18 said, **...I will show you my faith by my works.** If James can, Fred can.

Verses 19-26:

> You believe that there is one God. You do well. Even the demons believe—and tremble! But do you want to know, O foolish man, that faith without works is dead?
>
> Was not Abraham our father justified by works when he offered Isaac his son on the altar? Do you see that faith was working together with his works, and by works faith was made perfect? And the Scripture was fulfilled which says, "Abraham believed God, and it was accounted to him for righteousness." And he was called the friend of God. You see then that a man is justified by works, and not by faith only.
>
> Likewise, was not Rahab the harlot also justified by works when she received the messengers and sent them out another way? For as the body without the spirit is dead, so faith without works is dead also.

Now, that was the *New King James Version*, and it kept using the term *works*, and that word *works* is an unclear word to us in modern English usage. We usually only think of works relative to "good" or "bad," so I want to give you another translation that I think will clarify it for you.

James 2:14-26 (Weymouth):

> What good is it, my brethren, if a man professes to have faith, and yet his actions do not correspond? Can such faith save him? Suppose a Christian brother or sister is poorly clad or lacks daily food, and one of you says to them, "I wish you well; keep yourselves warm and well fed," and yet you do not give them what they need; what is the use of that? So also faith, if it is unaccompanied by obedience, has no life in it—so long as it stands alone.
>
> Nay, some one will say, "You have faith, I have actions: prove to me your faith apart from

corresponding actions and I will prove mine to you by my actions. You believe that God is one, and you are quite right: evil spirits also believe this, and shudder.

But, idle boaster, are you willing to be taught how it is that faith apart from obedience is worthless? Take the case of Abraham our forefather. Was it, or was it not, because of his actions that he was declared to be righteous as the result of having offered up his son Isaac upon the altar?

You notice that his faith was co-operating with his actions, and that by his actions, his faith was perfected; and the Scripture was fulfilled which says, "And Abraham believed God and his faith was placed to his credit as righteousness", and he received the name of God's friend.

You all see that it is because of actions that man is pronounced righteous, and not simply because of faith. In the same way also was not the notorious sinner Rahab declared to be righteous because of her actions when she welcomed the spies and hurriedly helped them to escape another way? For just as a human body without a spirit is lifeless, so also faith is lifeless if it is unaccompanied by obedience.

You have to have corresponding actions—actions that correspond to your faith. So all of these examples illustrate an action.

PART III

FAITH IS THE NUMBER ONE PRIORITY

8
Why Study Faith?

Now I want to deal with *why we ought to study the subject of faith*. Why make such a big issue out of it? I want to show you that faith is so vitally important to us that we need to understand *how it works*.

Romans 1:17:
> **For in it the righteousness of God is revealed from faith to faith; as it is written, "The just shall live by faith."**

Anything that you are called upon to live by certainly demonstrates its importance. If you are supposed to live by faith, how can you live by it effectively if you do not even know what it is? So, you need to know how it works and what it does if you are to live by it.

Notice this passage of Scripture says that the just shall live by faith. I am about to make a very important statement, and that is this: *Faith is a way of life. Faith is a way of living.*

God Declares Us Righteous

You will find the word *just* or a derivation of that word throughout the Bible. For instance, you will find just, justified, and justification. It literally means *to declare righteous.*[1]

When you accept Christ as God's remedy for sin—when you accept Christ as your personal living Savior and Lord, God declares you righteous.

---

[1]*Vine's Expository Dictionary of Old and New Testament Words*, (Grand Rapids: Fleming H. Revell, 1981), s.v. "Justification, Justifier, Justify," "A. Nouns," "#2 Dikatoma," p. 284.

Righteousness—that is a big-sounding word. And we do not hear, see, or use the word very much in everyday conversation. We could get into some discussion on the word *righteous* or *righteousness*, but I think it would be good to give you a simple, succinct definition of righteousness.

What does it mean? The simplest definition of righteousness is, *right-standing with God*. This definition comes from the definition of *justification*, above. Obviously, if I have been declared *righteous* by God, I must have *right-standing* with God and not *wrong-standing* any longer, because of the blood of Jesus.

Many people throughout the years have thought that righteousness was something that we as Christians had to do. For instance, a way that you live, a way that you dress, a way that you wear your hair, or something like that. Righteousness was considered some external thing that you do.

Actually, people really confuse two words, *righteousness* and *holiness*. Holiness has to do with the quality of your life lived on a daily basis. In other words, holiness is something you are responsible for.

On the other hand, righteousness is God's responsibility. There is absolutely nothing that you can do to make yourself *more* righteous. God has to make you righteous.

Sometimes people say, "How do you stand with so-and-so? I heard you had a falling out. I heard you had an argument. How do you stand with so-and-so?"

How do you stand with God? Righteousness is simply right-standing with God.

When Adam, in the Garden of Eden, disobeyed God, he caused a breach in the relationship of God and man. In other words, they *fell out*. God and Adam fell out—not really God, but Adam did it. As a result, it broke the lines of communication.

Consequently, man was actually—through Adam—declared by God as unrighteous, and unrighteousness is simply righteous with the prefix *un* which means non-righteous. So when Adam sinned, he caused the whole human race to become unrighteous—out of fellowship with God. No communication with God.

Jesus came, and through His sacrificial death, burial, and resurrection, brought man back into a position that enables him to have right-standing with God. It is called righteousness. So when you accept Christ as your personal Savior and Lord, God certifies you righteous.

Righteousness Means Paid in Full

Have you ever been somewhere and bought something and had to sign your name on a receipt or invoice? After signing, the agent or salesperson takes their stamper and stamps it "Paid in Full." That is your copy or receipt. They cannot come back on you and say you owe them any money. You have the receipt that says, *Paid in Full*.

In a similar manner, God stamps you righteous, and Satan, through intimidation or through bringing you low self-esteem, cannot legally come against your life and tell you that you owe anything, because you have been declared righteous by God. So righteousness means right-standing with God.

How do I stand with God? I stand fine with God. He is my Daddy, my Abba Father, and we are in right relationship.

Romans 1:17:

For in it the righteousness of God is revealed from faith to faith; as it is written, "The just shall live by faith."

So, if you are the righteousness of God in Christ, you should be living by faith. How often do you live by faith?

Once a week, once a month, Mother's Day, Father's Day, Easter, Thanksgiving, Christmas? How often do you live? Every day! So if the just shall live by faith, then it is saying that I ought to be living *by faith* every day.

If I am supposed to live by faith, I had better know what it is and what it is not, and I need to know how it works so that I can live by it, since that is what God requires of me. That is a very important reason to study and understand the subject of faith. Why? Again, because God requires me to live by faith.

Faith Is a Fight

Faith is a way of life. It is the God-kind of life. Look at the first part of First Timothy 6:12:

Fight the good fight of faith....

That is a very important statement. God through Paul is telling us to what? Fight. There are several things here that are very important to us. First of all, it tells us that we are in a fight. And you are in it whether you want to be in it or not.

The first reason you are in a fight is because of being born into this world as a human. Then, of course, when you became a Christian, that amplified the situation. Because if you stop and think about it, all life is a fight. Even non-Christian lives are a fight.

However, the only fight that Christians are called upon to fight is the fight of faith. That is all. You are not called upon to fight anything else. Now, you can get hurt fighting. You can get your nose broken. You can get bloody fighting. Fighting is work. Right? But He tells us to fight.

He says something else. He says fight the *good* fight. Now how in the world can fighting be good? Well, it is good when you win. That tells me that my Father is not calling upon me to fight a fight where I am supposed to get whipped. He did not say fight the fight of faith. He said, **Fight the *good* fight** because He wants you to win.

It is always a good game when our team wins. It is always a good fight when our fighter wins. Right? If our team lost, you would say, "Man, that was a bad game. That was a terrible game." That Scripture represents that same principle. God wants you to win. And everything that is necessary for you to win with, is provided for you in the Word of God. But you have to know it, and know how to activate it by your faith, or else you are going to get whipped.

Instead of fighting the good fight, you are going to get your backside kicked and your head whipped if you do not understand and know how to operate in faith. Life through Satan will beat you to death. And there will be nothing God can do about it because He has already done it. He says, **Fight the good fight of faith.**

Christians Are Not Called To Fight the Devil

The only fight that you are in is a faith fight. You are not fighting churches. You are not fighting preachers. You are not even called upon to fight the devil. You are not even supposed to fight demons, because number one, you could not even whip a baby demon with both of his eyes blindfolded, one of his legs in a cast and an arm in a sling. Why? Because a demon is a spirit creature. You cannot see one, so how are you going to fight him?

We do not have to fight Satan, because Satan is already defeated. Jesus fought him for us. His victory was actually our victory. Jesus never fought Satan to see who was the champion. He fought in our stead because He was the champion. He took our place in the ring. He fought for us. His victory is our victory.

You cannot find one Scripture in the Bible that tells you to fight the devil. In fact, you find just the opposite.

Satan is a bully and a super con man. If he can, he will con you into thinking that he has some kind of power over you, and that he can play with your life whenever he wants to, and you have to take it. But from the standpoint of the Word of God, he is already defeated.

Mark 16:17:

And these signs will follow those who believe: In My name they will cast out demons; they will speak with new tongues.

Believers Have Authority Over Satan

Are you a believer? Then Jesus is talking to you.

He did not say fight demons. He did not say shoot them. He said *cast them out*. That means throw them out. You could not throw them out if you did not have authority to throw them out, right? Right.

Luke 10:19:

Behold, I give you the authority to trample on serpents and scorpions, and over all the power of the enemy, and nothing shall by any means hurt you.

The word *power* in this verse is the Greek word *dunamis*,[1] which means ability. Let us read it that way:

Behold, I give you the authority (which literally means right, or privilege) **to trample on** (which means to walk on) serpents and scorpions, and over all the power (or ability), **of the enemy, and nothing shall by any means hurt you.**

Authority is greater than ability. I would much rather have authority than ability, because I can do more with

---

[1] James Strong, *The New Strong's Exhaustive Concordance of the Bible*, (Nashville: Thomas Nelson Publishers, 1984) p. 24 #1411.

authority than with ability. Ability could be limited by my physical size, IQ, perhaps, unfortunately, even the color of my skin. But if I have authority, it transcends all the rest of those things.

Behold, I give you the authority to trample on (walk on) **serpents....**

Now the words *serpents* and *scorpions* refer to Satan's imps. These words are being used symbolically or metaphorically. But wait a minute, if you are walking on something, no matter what you are walking on, it must be under your feet, right? If it is under your feet, that means you are on top of it, because your feet are at the lower extremity of your anatomy.

Behold, I give you the authority to trample on (walk on) **serpents and scorpions, and over all the *power*** (ability) **of the enemy, and nothing shall by any means hurt you.**

Now what is that talking about? Have you ever been doing something, perhaps sewing, and you stuck yourself with a needle? It felt good, right? No, it hurt. But you know, when you got stuck with that needle that was not the end of your life, was it? It did not kill you, did it? And guess what, it healed up soon, right? So when it says nothing shall hurt you, it means nothing shall hurt you in a permanent way.

In other words, the devil cannot legally put hurting on you that can remain. Wait a minute—it said, **Fight the good fight of faith.** You can get hit in a fight, and it can hurt you when you get hit. Given time, it will heal up and you will never even know you were hit. That is what He is talking about.

I am establishing the fact that you are not fighting the devil. Now, I will say this. Satan is our enemy personified, meaning that he is a person. So as far as being a person, he is the enemy. However, he is not our problem. He is not a Christian's problem.

Ephesians 4:27:

> Nor give place to the devil.

Now, wait a minute. Why would God tell us to do something that we were unable to do? Why would He hold out to us the impossible dream? That would not be in the character of God to do that, to require us to do something that He very well knows we are incapable of doing.

If He tells us to not give place to the devil, that means that the devil cannot have a place in our lives unless we *give* it to him. It is possible for us to give him that place by a consent of ignorance, by not knowing that we are giving it to him.

Do you like flies in your house? Have you ever found a fly in your house? Now, apart from there being a hole in the screen or something like that, I have only experienced letting a fly in the house by opening the door. But that was not my intent when I opened the door. My intent was to let me in. But the fly took advantage of my not knowing that he was following behind me. So, when I opened the door for Fred to go in, here comes the fly.

That is what I mean by a consent of ignorance. You might not realize what you are doing. If you open the door, the flies are coming in. You open the right breach in your life and the devil is coming in.

James 4:7:

> **Therefore submit to God. Resist the devil and he will flee from you.**

Most people, when quoting James 4:7 say, "Resist the devil and he will flee from you." But that is not what the verse says. It says,

> **Therefore submit to God.** (Then...) **Resist the devil and he will flee....**

Therefore submit to God. And you know what is sad?

The reason the devil has given Christians so much hell, is because most Christians are not submitted to God.

How do you submit to a God that you cannot see? The way that you are submitted to God is by being submitted to His Word, because God and His Word are one.

What would happen to you if you worked for a company and your boss sent you a memo by his secretary giving you some instructions to carry out and you refused to carry them out? What would that be? Insubordination— right? Because you are not submitted to your boss.

If you are submitted to your boss, you are submitted to the memo, because the memo came from the boss. Right? Well, God has sent you a memo directly from head office. The secretary, the Holy Spirit, delivered it, and here it is, the Bible, God's Word.

He says, **Therefore submit to God.** Submit yourself to the Word, then and only then do you have the right to resist the devil. It does not say fight him. It says resist him. And the Bible says he will flee from you. So you see that you are in a fight, but it is a faith fight—not a devil, demon or people fight, but a faith fight.

Now, remember that Satan—the devil—is the enemy. There is no question about that. He is the enemy personified. He is our enemy and we are his enemy. However, Satan is not after you. He cares nothing about you. You mean absolutely zero to him. You are unimportant. You do not count.

You may say, "Yes, Dr. Price, but why does he come after me and shoot at me all the time? How come the demons are trying to take me out?" Because the only thing about you that is important to Satan and demons is your faith. That is all, because that is all you have to win with.

He will attack your family, your marriage, your finances, your business, your profession, even your physical body with sickness or disease. But he really does not care about you or your body. All he wants to do is separate you from your faith. If he can separate you from your faith and cause your faith to be inoperative, he will then have control over your life.

Your faith is up for grabs. That is why the Boss says, **Fight the good fight of faith**. The only thing that makes you dangerous to Satan is your faith.

If you stop and think about it, it is the same in the natural realm. It is not the person who is the problem, it is the AIDS virus. It is the contagion, not the person. The person is irrelevant. If the person did not have the contagion, there would be no problem. The person has the contagion—the disease. It is the disease that is the problem, not the person. But persons are carriers of disease, and so are Christians carriers of faith. Can you relate to that?

Your faith in the spirit realm, to Satan, is just like AIDS or tuberculosis to a human in the natural realm. That is what makes you dangerous—your faith. That is the reason why the devil did not bother you before you received the Holy Spirit and started speaking with other tongues and became part of a church where you are taught to walk by faith and not by sight. Before that, you never had any problems with the devil. Why? Because the devil is trying to intimidate you, back you down and get you separated from your faith.

Before, he did not have to shoot at you, because he already had you in his bag. You were no threat to his kingdom. You did not know you had any authority, so why should he waste ammunition on a non-essential target? You only shoot at targets that are a problem for you.

He did not shoot at you until you started getting in line with the Word, because that is when you pose a danger to him. You are getting a *contagion*. Satan has to "quarantine" you, so to speak, because if he lets you loose, you are going to contaminate everyone with a faith bug—a faith virus.

I will prove this by Scripture.

1 John 5:4:

> **For whatever....**

Actually I think we need to adjust that word to what it means in today's language, because a *whatever* cannot be born of God. You see, a *whatever* could be a tree, or a cat, or a dog, or a mountain. I think we ought to substitute it with the word *whosoever*, because it is really talking about a whosoever.

For (whosoever) **is born....** Oh my, look at that! Read these words out aloud: "I am a whosoever." You are a whosoever.

Look closely—it does not say, "For whosoever is white, whosoever is black, whosoever has slanted eyes, whosoever is a pygmy, whosoever is educated bookwise, whosoever is talented, whosoever can sing like a sparrow, whosoever can run like an antelope, whosoever can be strong like a gorilla." It says, *whosoever*. Say aloud: "*Whosoever* means me!"

> **For whatever** *(whosoever)* **is born of God** (Are you born of God?) **overcomes the world...** (Are you a world overcomer?).

Satan Is the god of This World

What does *the world* mean? We think of the world as planet earth. It is not talking about the physical planet, terra firma. It is talking about the world system over which Satan presides. Satan is called, **the god of this world** (2 Cor. 4:4). Not the God of all the ages. But he is a god of this world system. That is why it is so messed up.

I certainly hope you do not think that God is running the world. If He is running the world, I do not want to go to heaven. Never, ever! This world down here is a grand, glorious mess. It is in chaos. It is a bomb getting ready to explode.

God is not running the world. God is running the Church. Satan is running the world system. But, like a boat in water, you are in this world system. So you have to survive in it. You have to function in it. God has given us the resources to overcome it, in the sense that it cannot, I repeat, it *cannot* stop you from fulfilling your destiny—and I am talking about fulfilling it in grand style. I am not talking about just making it with a welfare check.

For whatever (whosoever) **is born of God overcomes the world. And this is the victory that has overcome the world—our faith.**

That is how you overcome. That is why faith is so important. That is why God has commissioned me to stress the message of faith like I do, because that is the way you win. That is why Satan comes against your life, your family, your business, your profession—whatever it might be—to separate you from your faith. If Satan can separate you from your faith, he will destroy you.

Read it again: **For whatever** (whosoever) **is born of God overcomes the world. And this is the victory** (Oh, I love it. This is the what? Victory!) **that has overcome the world—our faith**. (Not *us*, but our *faith*.) That is why your faith is so important.

Satan is after your faith. He is not after you, he is after your faith, because that is how you win—with your faith.

Maybe that is why so many of you are getting your behinds kicked, and your heads whipped, and cannot make it in life, because you have not taken the time to develop your faith.

9

Faith Tested Produces Patience

James 1:1-3:

James, a bondservant of God and of the Lord Jesus Christ, To the twelve tribes which are scattered abroad: Greetings.

My brethren, count it all joy when you fall into various trials (temptations or tests), **knowing that the testing of your faith produces patience.**

I have said this before, but I want to say it again, because it bears repetition—that in the original writing, the Bible was written in scrolls, not in books like we have it today. Over the years these scrolls were collected, put together in what is called the *canon of Scriptures*, which is accepted as God's Word and made into a book.

When they were originally written in scrolls, they were written in continuous, narrative form, which means there were no chapter divisions, no punctuation marks, no chapter designations, no capitalized letters or small case differences. They were all written in the same type style. Whether capital letters or small case letters, there was no differentiation between the two.

When the translators put the Bible (the scrolls) together, in order to make it a lot easier to find things, they decided to make chapter divisions and number the verses. They also added the punctuation marks and the capitalization and small case designations.

The words were given by the Holy Spirit, but all those other things were given or put in there by man. I said all that to say this: because the translators did that, the flow of understanding can be broken. James 1:1-3 is a classic example of this.

What I want to do here is drop the numeral *two* next to **my brethren**. Also, the numeral *three* next to **knowing** in the third verse. Drop the punctuation marks, and you will see what a difference it makes.

It would then read like this: *My brethren count it all joy when you fall into various trials* (temptations or tests) *knowing that....*

The numerals three and two and the punctuation rob us of this tremendous revelation. If you read it as it is punctuated, you get the idea that God is masochistic because he would be saying, ...**count it all joy when you fall into various trials**...(temptations or tests).

There is nothing joyful about being tempted. Nothing! It is not joyful, and it is exceedingly difficult to count it all joy if you *do not know **that**.* This is the key: *My brethren count it all joy when you fall into divers trials* (temptations or tests) *knowing that....* If you do not know **that**, you cannot count it joy.

Now notice, he did not say, "My brethren, it *is* joy.... He said, *Count* it joy. In modern English you could say, "Treat it as joy." "Consider it as joy." "Act like it is joy." Can you relate to that? That is what he is saying. He says, *My brethren, (act) like it is all joy when you fall....*

Now that word **fall** can be a trap word, because when we think of somebody falling into temptations and trials, we think of them as being victimized, tricked or seduced.

When someone falls into something, we think of it in a negative way. That is not what this word means. A better way to say it would be, "My brethren, count it all joy when (you come into contact with, or when you come upon, or when you are faced with)...."

That is what it is talking about. The reason you know this is because it says, **My brethren, count it all joy when you fall into various trials....** The word *trials*, as I have noted before, also means temptations and tests. So whenever I read it, I always like to say temptations, trials and tests.

Temptations and Trials Will Come

He says, **My brethren, count it all joy when ye fall into divers temptations** (trials and tests)...(KJV). Now notice the word *when*. Notice it does *not* say: *My brethren, count it all joy (if) you fall....*

It does not say that. It says *when* you fall. That means you *will* fall. Now, understanding what the word *fall* means, what he is saying is, "You are *going to* come upon some temptations, trials and tests." There is no way you can avoid it other than dying, leaving this planet and going to heaven. If you live here you are going to be tempted, tried and tested.

Everyone is tempted, tried and tested. There is no immunity for anyone. He says, "*When* you (come upon these) temptations (trials and tests), count it all joy." But count it as joy knowing *that.* You cannot count it joy if you do not "know *that.*"

Now what is the *that* He wants us to know? He said, **...knowing *that* the *testing* of your faith....** Notice what is conspicuous in its absence; it does not say "the *testing* of *you.*"

Remember I told you that the only thing that makes you dangerous to the kingdom of darkness is your faith, and the only thing that Satan wants to do is separate you from your faith. You read it in First John 5:4 where it says:

> **...And this is the victory that *has* overcome the world—our faith.**

The Devil Wants Your Faith

If the devil can separate you from your faith, he has separated you from your ability to be victorious. If that is true, then he would have you right where he wants you. James says, **Knowing** *that* **the** *testing* **of your faith....**

Let me say it again—the devil does not care about you. You are unimportant. You are a cipher. You are a zero.

The temptations, the trials and the tests are like brush fires. They are like fires in one place with an alarm going off. He has your attention running to that place trying to put the fire out. While you are over there—"ring, ring, ring,"—there is another fire in another place, and you go running over there. When you are doing that, you are not exercising faith. You are getting caught up with the brush fires. You are getting caught up with the temptations, trials and tests.

That kind of thing is designed to get your attention off of the Word of God and on to the circumstances. If the devil can keep your attention on the circumstances, he will destroy you.

James says, **Knowing that the** *testing* **of your faith....** Let us personalize it. "Knowing that the *testing* of *my* faith...." Notice that he did *not* say the *testing* of *you*. He said, **Knowing that the testing of your faith.... Not *you*. Your** *faith*.

The devil does not want you—he wants your faith. But through the temptation, the trials and tests he will attack your body, your mind, your wife, your husband, your ministry, your business, your profession, your children, your parents.

What for? To get your attention on those issues and off of God's Word. If he can do that successfully, he can render you inoperative, helpless, and defeated. That is why this subject is so important.

Knowing that the testing of your faith....

Another interesting word here is the word *testing*, which is literally the word *proving*. So it is really saying this: "Knowing that the *proving* of your faith *produces* patience." The word *patience* literally means "endurance,"[1] or the ability to stand.

So it would read like this: "My brethren, count it all joy when you fall into *various trials*, (temptations *or tests*), knowing that the testing (proving) of your faith produces endurance." In other words, the ability to stand. You are in a war. *Fight the good fight of faith.*

You have to learn how to stand. Knowing that the *proving* of your faith.... Now who is that *proving* for? This should show you that God could not be the One responsible for the temptations, trials and tests, because He knows everything.

God has all knowledge about every man. Why would He waste our time, and His own time and resources, trying to prove something about us that His omniscience would already know? But, there are two people who do not know. Satan is one of them, and you are the other one.

Think about this. You do not really know what you can take and what you can stand and where you really are with your faith until the chips are down. When the sun is shining it is easy to say, "Glory to God, praise the Lord, Hallelujah." But can you praise Him and give Him glory when the doctor says you are going to die? When they say, "We can't fix it," where is *hallelujah, glory to God* and *praise the Lord* then?

Satan does not know you do not know, so he will pressure you to such a point that you break—break with the Word of God, and get caught up in the situation.

---

[1]James Strong, *Greek Dictionary of the New Testament, The New Strong's Exhaustive Concordance of the Bible*, (Nashville: Thomas Nelson Publishers, 1984), p. 24, #5281.

Satan Must Have An Open Door

You have to have a doorway open for the devil to get in. Without that open door he cannot put things on you. If he could, he would put cancer on every person in the world. He has no right to do anything to you, except what you let him do. Otherwise he would kill every one of us. Satan is our enemy and you are his enemy. The most logical thing to do would be to get rid of the enemy.

Why has Satan not killed every Christian? He cannot, without your cooperation and help. Whether you know it or not, you can help the enemy by a consent of ignorance. By being ignorant of certain things, you end up giving him comfort.

My wife, Betty, was attacked with cancer because of her lack of knowledge about some physical things that *she was not doing*. There was nothing wrong spiritually. But the devil got to her through a door she left open in the physical realm, because there were some things she *was not* doing—things she did not know were important. She was not taking care of herself in the way she should have, from a physical point of view, and it gave the enemy the opportunity to come against her. But we never wavered, because she knew what the Word said.

Understand this—we did not like any of the news we received. We are human, too, just like everyone else. You stick us with a pin and we bleed just like you do. But because we *knew* the Word, we had no fear about it. We had natural hurt and pain because we are human.

Pain hurts—I don't care who you are. In fact, you will be in serious trouble if you cannot feel pain (in the natural, that is), because pain is an alarm system to let you know something is wrong.

If you did not experience pain you would keep pushing forward until you break something. So the pain is an alarm to let you know something needs to be checked out. God built these things into your body. Satan will take advantage of these things and try to prostitute them and use them to destroy you.

So the devil does not know what you are going to do. That is why the temptations, trials and tests come.

We are the children of God. He is our heavenly Father. But He is in heaven and we are on the earth. It is His responsibility to train His kids. How does He train us? God is so clever, so smart; He has the devil working for Him, without the devil knowing it, and without pay.

Satan Is Our Trainer

Satan is our trainer, and he does not even know it! The devil thinks he is destroying us—and of course he will if you do not know how faith works—but if you learn how faith works, then the temptations, the trials and the tests will give you the opportunity to find out where you are in your faith.

God's purpose is that you use your faith to overcome every temptation, trial and test that comes against you. When you overcome something, you get stronger (or you should). You have to understand how I said that. I am not talking about this sick idea that some have come up with, that *God puts* things on you to make you a better person. He does not! In fact, all you have to do is obey His Word and you will never have to learn anything by trials and tribulations.

If you will take God's Word and use God's Word to step on and over the temptations, trials, and tests, you will not be harmed. It is in that exercise that you become stronger, and find out where you are faith-wise.

You think you know where you are, but not yet. You will find out when the doctor tells you, "We give you six months to live. There is nothing we can do for you." Then you will find out how much *praise the Lord, hallelujah,* and *glory to God,* you have. The temptations, trials and tests will allow your faith to be proved to you.

When I signed my name on the documents to purchase our present property (the former Pepperdine University property), it was for fourteen million dollars. But my faith had grown since signing to buy the first property in Inglewood, California. It only cost seven hundred fifty thousand dollars. We are talking about fourteen million dollars, as opposed to seven hundred fifty thousand dollars. When I put my hand on the pen for the seven hundred fifty thousand dollars, I thought I had the palsy! I am serious. But I understand that everything is relative.

At that time, to me, seven hundred fifty thousand dollars was like seven trillion dollars. I had never heard of that much money—in terms of *me* being involved with it. Do you understand what I mean? But, because of the seven-hundred-fifty-thousand-dollar deal and walking by faith over the years, when it came to the fourteen million dollars, I could sign my name on the document easier than I could for the seven hundred fifty thousand dollars. Why? Because I had been walking by faith over the previous years.

I knew what my faith could do. I knew where my faith was. My faith had been proved to me. You need to understand how important faith is. Why? Because it is the testing or proving of your faith.

Remember again, two people are involved—you and the devil. He does not know how important faith is, but God wants *you* to know. So the devil will use the temptations, trials and tests to destroy you, and God will allow him to. But God has given you the way out.

Do you understand what I am saying? Because if you do not understand what I am saying, you will get this idea that many in the Body of Christ have, when they say such things as, "Well, God put this on me to test me. God put this on me to make me a better person."

God Only Puts Victory on His Children

God is not putting anything on you but victory. Most of the time the only reason you learned the lesson through the hardship, was because your head was hard, and your behind was soft. You only have two ways to learn—listen to your teacher, or find it out the hard way! Because you *are* going to learn, it is guaranteed.

Remember this, experience is *not* the best teacher. But, if you do not listen to someone, sometime, somewhere, and some way, you *will* learn by experience. That is not the best way to learn. Learn by listening to someone else. Obedience is better than sacrifice.

All you have to do is go back and look at Israel. The only time they ever had to make a sacrifice was when they messed up. If they had stayed right, flew right all the time, then they would not have had to make a sacrifice. Remember this, *sacrifice is that which obedience would have prevented.* There would have been no need for the sacrifice if there had been obedience to the law.

I said it before, but I want to say it again, Satan will use the temptations, trials, and tests to destroy you—and God will allow him to. But God has given us the way out. You can see this clearly from First Corinthians 10:13:

> **No temptation has overtaken you except such as is common to man; but God is faithful, who will not allow you to be tempted beyond what you are able, but with the temptation will also make the way of escape, that you may be able to bear it.**

With that verse, you ought to know it is not God Who brings the temptations, trials and tests. If you took the way of escape, then you would have missed whatever lesson you were supposed to have learned by the temptation, trial and test. God is the One giving you the way of escape. It is the devil who tries to put it on you. Can you see that?

He said, **No temptation** *has overtaken* **you** *except* **such as is common to man; but God is faithful, who will not allow** (or permit) **you to be tempted** (tried or tested) *beyond what* **you are able....**

Now what is my ability? My ability is the Word of God through faith. There is not one single thing that the devil can bring against you that faith cannot handle, *if* you know how it works, and *if* you put it into operation. If you do not know, you are going down, because Satan is there to see that you go down.

The Way of Escape Is Provided

The way of escape is by taking God at His Word, by standing on that Word and making your confession of faith, and walking through the temptation, trial or test. You are in a fight of faith. Fight the good fight of faith, because you win.

God wants you to take His Word and knock those temptations, trials and tests in the head. Then and only then will you find out that the Word *really* works because you will have *experienced* it.

How do you know that the Word works? How do you know that God answers prayer? You can believe God answers prayers, because He says He does in His Word. But how do you *know* He will? You will never know until you get a prayer answered.

When I pray, I believe God is there. I believe God hears and I believe He will do what He says He will do. That is the basis on which I pray.

But you will never *know* that God will hear and answer prayer until you have had your prayer heard and answered. At that point, there is no one, nowhere, no how and no way, who can talk you out of the fact that God hears and answers prayer.

When that happens, you get as bold as a lion. This is when some of the other brothers and sisters will accuse you of being arrogant, because they do not know the difference between arrogance and confidence.

I am confident because I have been walking in the Word. However, some people who do not understand me, mistake my confidence for arrogance, and think I am a braggart.

I have been walking in the Word for more than twenty-five years. I am absolutely, positively, unequivocally convinced that God's Word works. You cannot talk me out of it. It is too late. I have the evidence! That is why I am so bold about it. Like it or lump it. Take it or leave it. *I know that I know that I know that my know "knows" that God does hear and answer prayer!*

How did I get there? By *acting* on the Word. How do I know that faith will move a mountain until I come face to face with one? How do I know that *with Jesus' stripes I was healed?* I know it when sickness tries to destroy my body, and I take God's Word and stand against it and destroy it with my faith. Then *I know* that I know that I know that *Himself took my infirmities and bore my sicknesses, and with His stripes I was healed!*

I started out by believing it, but *I did not know it until I experienced it.*

10

You Must Have Faith To Please God

Let us move on to something else relative to why we ought to study faith and why it is so important.

Hebrews 11:6:

> **But without faith it is impossible to please Him, for he who comes to God must believe that He is, and that He is a rewarder of those who diligently seek Him.**

Now, do not tell me that faith is not important and that you should not talk about it and study it. Look at verse 6 again:

> **But without faith it is impossible....**

Impossible means *not possible—no way*. If you cannot see from this statement in verse 6 how important the subject of faith is, I rest my case.

Faith Is More Important Than Love

As important as love is, the Bible never says that *without love it is impossible to please God*. The Bible tells us we ought to go to church—**not forsaking the assembling of ourselves together, as is the manner of some...** (Heb. 10:25). As important as it is to gather together as the children of God, nowhere does it ever say that without doing that, it is impossible to please God.

Faith Is More Important Than Tithing

You ought to bring all of your tithes into the storehouse.

Malachi 3:8,10:

> Will a man rob God? Yet you have robbed Me! But you say, "In what way have we robbed You?" In tithes and offerings...Bring all the tithes into the storehouse....

As important as that is (it is called *robbery* if you do not bring your tithes), it never says that without tithing it is impossible to please God.

Faith Is More Important Than Studying

2 Timothy 2:15:

> Be diligent to present yourself approved to God, a worker who does not need to be ashamed, rightly dividing the word of truth.

We ought to present ourselves approved to God. But as important as that is, nowhere does it ever say it is impossible to please God without doing it. Here and here alone, in Hebrews 11:6, in reference to faith, it says without this—*faith*—it is *impossible* to please God. And guess what? If you cannot please Him without faith, you certainly cannot get your prayers answered.

Let us go on, because there are some deep truths here that many people miss. Look again at Hebrews 11:6:

Faith Is Not Optional

> But without faith it is impossible to please Him, for he who comes to God must....

Underline the word *must*. The word *must* is an imperative necessity, meaning it is not an option.

> But without faith it is impossible to please Him, for....

I always substitute the word *because* for the word *for* since that is what it means. *For* is the old English way of talking. Since we do not talk that way today, it would read like this:

But without faith it is impossible to please (God), (because)...**he who comes to God must....**

Here is what is important: You do not *have* to come to God. You can go to hell. That is right, I said you can go to hell, and God will protect your right to go. In fact, God will marshal His angels around you to see to it that no one interferes with your transition from this life to hell. God will protect your right to go to hell, if that is what you choose. No one will be able to interfere with you going.

...he who comes to God must... is not saying you *have* to come to God. It is saying, *if* you make the choice to come to God, *if* you want to please Him, at that point, you have no options. Do you understand what I am saying?

One year my wife and I traveled to New York City for a television crusade. I had been to New York City many times, and I knew by experience that there were a number of airlines that would fly me out of Los Angeles International Airport to New York City.

If for some reason I did not like one airline, I had other options. But once I made my choice to fly on a particular airline which left at a particular time, I did not have any options if I wanted to get to New York City on that particular flight. I *must* be on board that plane when it lifts off the ground. Can you understand that? Do you understand that principle? That is what the writer is saying in Hebrews.

But without faith it is impossible to please Him, for (or, because) he who comes to God....

Very Few People Please God

I want to show you that there are only a handful of people who please God.

But without faith it is impossible to please Him, for (or, because) he who comes to God must believe that He is....

That is where most people stop reading. They say, "Oh, yes, hallelujah. Praise the Lord, glory to God. I believe that God is." And that is where they stop. I did it for seventeen years. That is where I stopped. I had committed the verse to memory. **For he who comes to God must believe that He is....** "Hallelujah, I believe," but I never read the rest of the verse.

> **But without faith it is impossible to please Him, for** (or, because) **he who comes to God must believe that He is, and that He is a rewarder of those who diligently seek Him.**

You have to believe *both* of those principles in order to please God. There are very few—ministers especially—who please God. The reason I know that is because they are the ones saying, "God put that on you, sister. God's testing you. God is trying you. Just hold on to God's unchanging hand. The Lord knows just how much you can bear."

Some of you have heard it before: "He won't put on you any more than you can bear."

You did not get that in school, you got it in church. You heard it from the preacher. I am here to tell you that cancer is not a reward. If it is, keep it. A heart attack is not a reward. AIDS is not a reward. A failed kidney is not a reward. A brain tumor is not a reward. If it is, do not reward me.

God Is a Rewarder

The Bible says God is a rewarder. My understanding of reward is the fact that you are the better for having received the reward, not the worse. Every time a hurricane, tornado, earthquake or tidal wave does great destruction, God is blamed. They call it "an act of God." He gets blamed for all the dirt, because they are ignorant—and unfortunately most preachers in the pulpit are ignorant. Ignorant of the Word. And so they blame God. They say, "God put that on you. God took him."

This is the kind of thing they say, even at the funeral, while a mother and children and relatives are sitting there crying their hearts out, hurt and destroyed because their loved one is gone.

That preacher—the one who ought to be giving them the truth, the one who ought to be giving them comfort, the one who ought to be telling them like it is, the one who should be giving them God's Word—will dare to stand there and say, "The Lord took him."

That is not true. God is not taking anyone. Now, it is true, He will let you go. If *you* let you go, *He* has no choice but to let you go. But God is not taking anyone. He did not take your mother, or your goldfish, or your dog, or your hog, or your cat. He did not take your brother, or your sister, or your child, or your father. God did not take them, and it is unscriptural to say that He did.

God Takes People Alive

I will show you Scripture where God took people. And every time God ever took anyone, He took them *alive*. Enoch went jogging one day and got out into the glory, into the anointing and just jogged right on into heaven. God took him. He did not die.

Elijah and Elisha were walking through the field one day—the prophet and the protégé. The protégé was talking to the prophet. He said, "I want a double portion of what you have." Elijah said, "I'll tell you what, if you see me when I go, you will have what you want."

Just about that time, the afternoon express came by. The heavenly chariot came down through the sky and a whirlwind picked up Elijah and took him up into heaven. He went alive, not dead.

And, of course, the Lord Jesus Himself went up into heaven alive, a cloud receiving Him from the Mount of Olives.

Let us look at one more Scripture on the importance of why you should study the subject of faith:

Hebrews 3:7-11:

Therefore, as the Holy Spirit says:

"Today, if you will hear His voice, do not harden your hearts as in the rebellion in the day of trial in the wilderness, where your fathers tested Me, tried Me, and saw My works forty years.

Therefore I was angry with that generation, and said, 'They always go astray in their heart, and they have not known My ways.' So I swore in My wrath, 'They shall not enter My rest.'"

God is speaking through the mouth of the writer of Hebrews, and taking us back to when Israel came out of Egypt, and God led them to the Promised Land. And they provoked God by their lack of faith.

Now the writer comes back and says to you and to me in verse 12:

Beware, brethren, lest there be in any of you an evil heart of unbelief....

Look at the revelation. Unbelief is *evil*. You think smoking cigarettes is evil, and it is. You think drinking alcohol is evil, and it is. You think shooting up with drugs is evil, and it is.

But look at this! Here is one thing that most people completely ignore. They do not mind disbelieving. They will go all over the place and disbelieve and think nothing about it.

God Calls Unbelief Evil

God calls unbelief *evil*. If you do not believe, you are operating in evil. Even if you never take a cigarette, never pop a pill, never shoot up any drugs, never steal anything, never use any profanity, God says you are operating in evil.

Hebrews 3:12-4:2:

> Beware, brethren, lest there be in any of you an evil heart of unbelief in departing from the living God;

> But exhort one another daily, while it is called "Today," lest any of you be hardened through the deceitfulness of sin. For we have become partakers of Christ if we hold the beginning of our confidence steadfast to the end, while it is said:

> "Today, if you will hear His voice, do not harden your hearts as in the rebellion."

> For who, having heard, rebelled? Indeed, was it not all who came out of Egypt, led by Moses? Now with whom was He angry forty years? Was it not with those who sinned, whose corpses fell in the wilderness?

> And to whom did He swear that they would not enter His rest, but to those who did not obey? So we see that they could not enter in because of unbelief.

> Therefore, since a promise remains of entering His rest, let us fear lest any of you seem to have come short of it. For indeed the gospel was preached to us as well as to them; but the word which they heard did not profit them, not being mixed with faith in those who heard it.

You have to mix God's Word with faith. If you do not mix it with faith, it is not going to do you any good. Look at verse 2 again:

> For indeed the gospel was preached to us as well as to them....

The *gospel* is the Word of God. *But the Word preached did not profit them.* You can *hear* it and it not profit you. If it did not profit you, it did you no good. You might as well not have heard it. God's Word is supposed to profit you. You are supposed to be the better for it. Let us continue with verse 2:

> For indeed the gospel was preached to us as well as to them; but the word which they heard did not profit them....

...did not profit them.... They heard the Word. That confirms exactly what James said when he said, **But be doers of the word, and not hearers only...** (James 1:22).

The Word Must Be Mixed With Faith

It is possible to hear the Word and yet not be a doer. Faith can come because faith always comes when what? *You hear.* Because faith comes by what? Hearing, and hearing by the Word of God. Notice again:

> **For indeed the gospel was preached to us as well as to them; but the word which they heard did not profit them, not being mixed with faith....**

Where?

> **..in those who....**

What?

> **...heard it.**

It is *my* responsibility to mix it. I have to mix God's Word with faith. Now how do you mix God's Word with faith? How do I mix it? Well, just think of the Word "mix." If you have ever baked a cake you ought to be able to relate to this word *mix* very easily.

When you mix, you blend things together. You do not leave the butter on the countertop on the other side of the sink, and the vanilla flavoring on the side of the sink, and the flour sitting by the dining room table.

Mix Means Blend

Mix means blend. *Blend* means put them together. It means that when it is finished, you cannot tell where the butter is, where the vanilla is or where the flour is. It all looks like one mass of dough. Is that correct?

He says it has to be mixed with faith—not butter, but *faith*—and it has to be mixed in them that hear it. How do you mix a cake batter? There are about three basic ways to mix something. You can either put it in a mixing machine with two beater blades and a mixing bowl attached; or, you can have a small hand-held mixer; or you could do it the old-fashioned, reliable way by using a spatula or a large spoon.

You have to mix God's Word with faith when you hear it, and you have to do it in your spirit, or in your heart. How do you do it? Well, you do not use a literal mixing bowl—but you really *do* use a mixing bowl. The mixing bowl is your mouth, and the beater blade is your tongue.

The Word Is Mixed by Speaking

You mix God's Word by *speaking* God's Word. That is the way you mix it. That is why you always hear me talking the Word.

Sometimes people who do not understand what I am doing will criticize me. What they do not realize is that I am in the process of mixing—I am in the mixing mode. Praise God! I am mixing my faith with the Word. That is what is producing the results.

Maybe if you do the same thing you will have the same results. Speak the Word. Do not talk the circumstances, talk the solution. Do not talk what you see, talk what God says about what you see. That is what will change the circumstances.

The Scriptures that you have already covered were designed to show you how important faith is, and how important it is that you study faith.

PART IV

THE DYNAMICS OF FAITH

11
All Believers Have Faith

Another important aspect of the subject of faith is to understand and know you do, in fact, have faith. The challenge is not the need of more faith, but to know how it works.

I know that most of you have never prayed this prayer that I am going to illustrate. I prayed this way because of my lack of knowledge when I first got saved. I am sorry to say the churches I was involved with then did not teach me. They preached at me and preached to me, but they did not teach me. This is not a criticism, but rather an observation.

Ignorance Destroys Faith

I used to pray a very ignorant, stupid, dumb, non-sensical prayer. I am sure there are probably not too many people reading this book who have prayed something as dumb as what I prayed, but I used to pray this prayer with tears. I was really sincere about it. I used to pray, "Lord, give me more faith."

I know that you have heard people pray that prayer. I was dumb. I did not know. When you do not know, you do not know, and that is a tragedy. I used to pray, "Lord, give me more faith."

Here was my rational. I figured if I had enough faith, things would work. They would work positively, they would work in my favor and I would be blessed of God. But everything I did in life was a struggle. I mean my struggles had struggles. Every day, when the clock came on, instead of waking up and saying, "Good morning, Lord," I would wake up and say, "Good Lord, it's morning."

I am serious. God is my witness—it was hard, and I figured if I could ever get enough faith things would work. Now it is amazing that intrinsically something on the inside let me know that faith was the key, but I did not know why I knew that it was, and I did not know what to do about it. So the only thing I thought I could do about it was to ask God to give me more of it. I figured if I ever got enough, I would know that I had enough, because it would work— but it never worked.

Christians Don't Need More Faith

Many years later, fortunately, I found out that the problem was not that I needed more of it. I just needed to know how it worked. I needed to know that I had it, and *you* need to know that *you*, as a believer, have it too.

Every person who has ever done what Romans 10:9 says—that is, confess with your mouth Jesus as Lord and believe in your heart that God raised Him from the dead— is saved. That constitutes what we call salvation, or being born again, or becoming a new creature in Christ Jesus. Those are just different ways of talking about the same thing. If you have ever experienced that, *you have faith, and you have enough faith*. You do not need any *more* of it, you just need to know what to *do* with it.

When you know what to do with it, it will grow and expand, and get stronger. You simply need to know that you have it, when you received it, and how it came. It is in the Bible and you need to know that you know that you know that you have it. That way you can put it on the shelf and you do not have to deal with it again, because you will know that you have it. From that point on, you can set about to develop it and move on in to the higher things of God. God wants you to progress to greater heights.

You need to know your origin, in faith. If you do not know you had a point of origin, or know where you began, or that you are somebody in God and that you *have* faith, then you will never be able to rise above your present level.

You need to go back and establish for yourself, once and for all, that you are somebody, that you came from somewhere, that you have the faith of God, and that you know that you know that you have it. That way the devil can never, ever, intimidate us through the circumstances or back us down and cause us to live below our privileges.

Every Believer Has Faith

Romans 12:3:

> **For I say, through the grace given to me, to everyone who is among you, not to think of himself more highly than he ought to think, but to think soberly, as God has dealt to each one a measure of faith.**

Now underline the words **to each one** a measure of faith. How many are left out of **each one**? It did not say that God has dealt to some. It said that God has dealt to **each one**, and the words *each one*, are generic. It means human, male and female. God has dealt to *each one* a measure. What connotation does that word *measure* bring to mind? Amount, quantity, or degree, right? A measure can be increased or decreased. Can you agree with that?

Notice what it does *not* say. It does not say that God has dealt to each one *faith*. (Note: *The New King James Version* says, **a measure**, but the *King James Version* says, **the measure**, which I prefer, because it implies a definite amount, whereas **a measure** implies that different persons may have different amounts dealt to them.

God Is No Respecter of Persons

One person may have a pint, but someone else may have a quart. That would not fit the character of God, because His Word says He is no respecter of persons. Since He requires us to live by faith, it would be unfair to give us different amounts because we would be at a disadvantage if we had less faith than someone else.

There is an implication here. The word *measure* alerts us to the fact that what God dealt us can be increased. Before we go further, I need to qualify something. When it says **each one**, it implies that everybody in the world has faith because that is exactly how we would have to interpret it.

You have to understand that the Bible is not written to everyone in the world. Everyone in the world can ultimately come to the place where the Bible can affect their lives positively, but the Bible is a coded book written to a certain class of people, namely, the people of God. Anyone who is not a child of God cannot understand the Bible. In other words, they can never know its message.

So when it says, **each one**, we need to qualify that it is not talking about each one in the world. Everyone does have natural human faith, but we are not talking about that—we are talking about the God-kind of faith. The kind of faith that comes from God.

The Word Must Be Rightly Divided

Let me show you an apparent contradiction in the Bible in reference to faith.

2 Thessalonians 3:2:

> **And that we may be delivered from unreasonable and wicked men; for not all have faith.**

You just read that **God has dealt to *each one* the measure of faith** (KJV). And there it says,

> **...for not all have faith.**

This is the way the superficial reader of the Bible comes up with the brilliant deduction that the Bible contradicts itself, because he does not understand what he is reading. If you look at Romans 12:3 and then look at this, it is a definite contradiction, *if* the writer is talking about the same thing in both places. But he is not. That is why the Bible says, **...rightly dividing the word of truth** (2 Tim. 2:15). That implies you could *wrongly* divide it.

And that we may be delivered from unreasonable and wicked men....

Unreasonable and wicked men would not be talking about the saints of God. It is not talking about the children of God—about born-again people. That verse is talking about sinners. They do not have the God-kind of faith. He is right. They do not. In Romans 12:3 he is talking about children of God. Now, how do you know that? Just because Fred Price says so? No! Let us find out how you know.

Romans 1:7:
To all who are in Rome....

If you put a period there, then you would know that this letter is a letter addressed to how many people? Everyone in Rome. But it does not have a period there, so you would read it like this:

To all who are in Rome, beloved of God, called to be saints....

So that tells us this letter has a limited purpose. It is not an open letter to everyone in Rome. It is only to those who are beloved of God and called to be saints. It is only written to the Christian community, only to those who are called to be saints. Now, with that in mind, let us look again at Romans 12:3. I want to give you the Frederick K. C. Price paraphrase edition of that third verse, keeping in mind what you just read in chapter 1 verse 7.

For I say, through the grace given to me, to everyone who is among you (saints at Rome), **not to think of himself more highly than he ought to think, but to think soberly, as God hath dealt to each one** (among you saints at Rome) **a measure of faith.**

Can you see that? Now, you have a dilemma, because you are not in Rome. This is great for the Romans, but what about us? You are two thousand years removed from Rome. Well, all you have to do is ask yourself the question: how many churches are there? Only one. How many Bodies of Christ are there? Just one. How many heads of the church are there? One.

If you are in *the* Body of Christ, you have to be in *the* same Body of Christ that the Romans were in. Therefore, if God dealt to the Romans a measure of faith, He would have to have dealt that same measure of faith to you, because the Bible says that God is no respecter of persons. Therefore, if He dealt the Romans a *measure* of faith and did not deal that measure of faith to you, then He would in fact be a respecter of persons.

That means you have the same measure of faith the Romans had. Now the question is, where did you get it? How did you get it? When did it come? Good questions.

Ephesians 2:8:
For by grace you have been saved through faith, and that not of yourselves; it is the gift of God.

Notice it says,

For by grace you have been saved....

How?

...through faith....

Through what? *Faith!*

...and that not of yourselves; it is the gift of God.

Now, here is how most people interpret that. They say, "Okay, John 3:16 says, **For God so loved the world that He gave His only begotten Son.**" So you could say that Jesus was a what from God? Gift! So when people read Ephesians 2:8, they say, "That's right, Brother Price, salvation is a gift."

May I suggest to you, that is not what he is talking about here? He is not talking about salvation. He is not talking about Jesus. Look at it very carefully. It says,

For by grace you have been saved through faith....

He is talking about *faith*.

For by grace you have been saved through faith, and that (faith is) **not of yourselves; it** (that faith) **is the gift of God.**

He is talking about the faith to get salvation. You have to have the faith first in order to get salvation, because it says, **For by grace you have been saved *through* faith**. You have to have faith present to go *through* it to get the salvation.

Faith Comes By Hearing

Now, how does God get that faith to you? Romans 10:17 says, **So then faith comes by hearing, and hearing by the word of God**. Faith comes by what? *Hearing*. That is why Jesus said in the sixteenth chapter of the gospel of Mark, verse 15, **...Go into all the world and preach** (*preach* means verbally proclaim) **the gospel to every...** (God has dealt to each one a measure of faith) **creature**.

Could this be the way God deals faith to us, by preaching the Word? Faith comes by hearing. Go into all the world, and preach the Gospel to every creature. Why Jesus? Because faith comes by hearing and hearing by the Word of God. If you do not preach the Word, faith cannot come, and if faith cannot come, they cannot hear. If they cannot hear, they cannot believe. If they cannot believe, they cannot receive, and if they cannot receive, they are going to hell.

Faith Comes By the Preaching of the Gospel

Preach the Word. Faith will come. They can believe and they can receive. I submit that the way God deals faith to each one is by preaching the Gospel to each one. That is how your faith came—when you heard God's Word—even if you were in a hotel room contemplating suicide, and happened to open one of the drawers in the dresser and found a copy of the Gideon Bible. You picked it up and it fell open to John 3:16.

Even though there was no one in that room, you heard something down on the inside of you. Your own spirit man said, **For God so loved the world**, and that was the key. That was the catalyst and you got saved. Did you know that you can hear on the inside as well as on the outside? Faith comes by what you hear, whether it is by your spirit, by the Holy Spirit, or whether it is by the proclamation of the Word of God through the mouth of a minister. *Faith comes by hearing*!

That is how God dealt faith to you—by preaching the Word to you. Can you understand that? That is how God did it, by the proclamation of the Word. That is why the preaching of the Word is so important to the sinner. Once the sinner gets the Word and gets saved, then he needs to find out how faith works. But that is how you got your faith, the day that you accepted Christ, the day that you heard the Word of God concerning Jesus as Savior and Lord. That is when God dropped the measure of faith into your spirit.

It became yours and for some of you, it has been sitting there like a seed doing nothing for the last twenty-five years, only because you did not know what to do with it. You went to church where they did not tell you anything. So you have been struggling through life trying to make it on your own smarts. That is why it is such a shambles. You have not been relying on God, because you did not know how to rely on God by faith. Many people think I have great faith—or let me say it this way, they think that I have more faith than they do. That is why they want me to pray for them.

But here is the good news. I do not have any more faith than you do, and you do not have any more faith than I do. You all have been dealt the same measure of faith. That is why I like dealing with my heavenly Father, because He puts all of us on par. Nobody has any advantage or disadvantage over anyone else.

12
How Faith Works

We will now proceed to the actual mechanics of how faith works.

Hebrews 11:1:

> Now faith is the substance of things hoped for, the evidence of things not seen.

I call this the technical, traditional, biblical definition of faith. I am sure that many of you actually know this verse by memory. If you do, I want you to quote it out loud so that you hear yourself.

After you have said that, what did you say? Remember this, you cannot apply definitions to circumstances. You have to extract from the definition what the definition actually means and then apply it to the circumstances.

You cannot contract a disease and then stand over the disease and say, **Now faith is the substance of things hoped for, the evidence of things not seen.** That will do no good. You are absolutely right, but a *definition* is not going to change your circumstances. It is true that **faith is the substance of things hoped for, the evidence of things not seen,** but what does all that mean? Let us find out.

Faith Has a Time

When I first got into this in terms of the Word of God, and the revelation came to me that faith was the key that operates everything in the Kingdom of God, I was impressed with the fact that faith has a time. There is a time when faith is faith, and there is a time when it is not, and you have to know the difference.

You have to know that you know *when* faith *is* and when it is not. For instance, I am sure you have heard people say, "Well, I know the Lord is going to make a way." Or, "Well, I know God is going to do..." thus and so.

When people say this, they are the epitome of sincerity. They mean it from their heart. "I know the Lord is able. I know God will make a way. I know God is going to do...." They were sincere when they said that, and they thought they were operating in faith because they said, "I know God is going to...." But what they did not understand was the *time* of faith.

This is one of the most important things you can ever learn about faith—its time. In other words, when is faith faith? I discovered right away that faith was *present tense*. Faith is always *now*. If it is not *now*, it is not faith.

When you say, "I know God is going to do something," you are saying that He has not done it. Therefore, that could not be present tense—it would have to be future tense. And God is not a future tense God. God is a now God! God is a present tense God. God will never move on behalf of, "I know that God is going to do something." Because when you say that God is going to do something, you have denied that He has *already* done it. You have to understand that.

Faith Is Present Tense

When I saw this **now**, I said, "There it is right there. There is the proof that I need to show that faith is present tense!" So I began to teach that. I knew faith had a *time*, so I began to teach that. Everywhere I went, I taught that faith is present tense and I used Hebrews 11:1, **Now faith is....**

A woman who was in one of my meetings wrote me a very nice letter and, in essence, said I was kind of dumb because I did not understand that the word N-O-W was not even in the original Greek text, and it was invalid for me to use that word *now* to prove that faith is *now.*

I am the kind of person who intends to be right. The only reason I am ever wrong is because I do not know that I am wrong. I figure if anyone on this planet can be right, Fred Price can be the one who is right. Understand how I am saying this. I want to be right. I do not know about you.

I cannot speak for you, I can only speak for me. I want to be right, not so that I can say that I am the only one right, not so I can shine over someone else. I just want to be right. I figure if anyone can be right, why not me? Is there a law that says Fred cannot be right?

I checked out what the lady said, because I know I do not know everything. I found out the woman was right. The N-O-W is not there. So I had a dilemma. I had to figure out, what am I going to do?

Since I cannot use this word *now* as an indicator of present tense, I had to find another word. I realized that the word *now* had to be replaced with a connective word like *but* or *therefore.* What that does is tie together the 39th verse of the tenth chapter with the first verse of the eleventh chapter. So it would read like this, reading verse 39:

> **But we are not of those who draw back to perdition, but of those who believe to the saving of the soul.**
> But **faith is the substance of....**

Or you could say,

> **But we are not of those who draw back to perdition, but of those who believe to the saving of the soul.**
> Therefore **faith is the substance of....**

So I said, "Okay, I know that faith is present tense. I know that faith is *now.* I know that if it is not now, it is not faith and it will not compute. So let me juggle this around."

I dropped the word *now*, capitalized the word *faith* and made it the first word of the verse. Then it would read like this, "Faith is...," "Faith is...." I said, "I am back in business, because *is* is present tense."

You could say, faith *was*. Past tense. You could say, faith *will be*. Future tense. But if you say, faith *is*, that cannot be past, and that cannot be future, it has to be what? *Now!*

I was back in business. I began to juggle it around a little more. I said, "Faith is." That is one statement. Then I said, "Let me compound this and say it this way: 'Faith is now.'" Or you could say it like this: "Now faith is." I do not care how you say it, it is still present tense. So, the first and most important thing you want to learn about faith is that faith is *always present tense*.

I want you to read this out loud so that you hear yourself reading it: *Faith is always present tense. If it is not present tense, if it is not now, it is not faith, and it will not work.*

Think about this again: when you say, "I know God is going to do something," that is not a statement of faith. That will never come to pass. It is commendable that you have that kind of belief that God is going to do something. But that is not faith. According to God's Word He has *already done it*.

You Have To Say What God Says

You have to say what God says if God's Word is to produce results in your circumstances. To be in faith, you have to agree with God. You cannot say you know "God is going to." For instance, Philippians 4:19 says, **And my God shall supply all your need....** What you have to say is, "Praise God, I believe that all my needs *are* met."

That becomes a confession of faith. That is what activates God's power on my behalf. That is present tense. Not *were* (past tense) met. Not, *going to be* (future tense). I believe that all my needs *are* met, because God said in His Word, **And my God shall supply.**

Take healing as an example. "Well, I'm believing God that He's going to heal me." Forget it! You had better find a good doctor or get the death certificate ready, because that is not a statement of faith. It is wonderful that you think that, but that is not faith, and the devil will kill you while you are making that kind of statement. He has a legal right to do it, because it is not a statement of faith.

"Well, I know God is able." That is not faith. "Well, I know the Lord is going to." No! That is not faith and it will not work. You have to say what God says. In reference to healing, God said, Matthew 8:17, **He Himself....** [And if you read the context, **He Himself** refers to Jesus Christ.] It says, **He Himself took....** (*Took* is a past tense designation.) It goes on to say, **He Himself took our infirmities and bore....** *Bore* is a past tense designation. If He took them and bore them, He must not want us to take them and bear them, so that makes us free.

First Peter 2:24 says, **...by whose stripes you were healed.** *Were* is past tense, indicative of the fact that the time of action has already taken place. It does not say, *By whose stripes you are being healed*. That would be present tense. It does not say, *By whose stripes you shall be healed*. *Shall be* is future tense. But He said, **...By whose stripes you were....** So if *you were, you are.* And if *you are, you "is,"* and **Now faith is.**

All the Promises of God Are Present Tense

You have to take all the promises of God and see them in the present tense. In the natural, I may be having challenges. In the natural, Satan may be trying to put something on me, but my response to that has to be what God says if God's power is to be released on my behalf. I have to say, "I believe I am healed."

Even when my temperature is 110, I have to say, "I believe I am healed." I do not deny that the temperature is 110. But when it comes to my faith, if I want God's power to be involved in my circumstances, I have to put it in the present tense. "I believe *I am* healed." I am not *being* healed, and I do not believe God is *going to*. I believe I am. That is present tense. That is faith. Anything other than that is not faith, and God is under no obligation to act on that.

Faith Is Not Sense

You may say, "Yeah, but that doesn't make sense." And you are absolutely right, it does not make sense, because it is not sense; it is faith. Faith is faith and sense is sense and dogs are dogs and hogs are hogs. Hogs are not dogs and dogs are not hogs and sense is not faith and faith is not sense.

You are absolutely right, it does not make sense. Because it does not say, *Now (sense) is the substance of things hoped for....* It says *faith* is. They are spelled differently and they have different meanings.

We will move on to the second thing we want to learn about faith. Hebrews 11:1 says,

Now faith is the substance of things hoped for....

We need a definition so we can be in agreement. What is "substance"? Most people would say: tangibility; materiality; assurance; guarantee.

Substance Can Be Contacted With the Senses

Those are good, but let me suggest a different definition and see if you can agree with it. *Substance* is that which can be contacted with your senses. Can you agree with that? It is something I can see, smell, taste, touch or hear. So, you could say it like this, *faith is the substance*, (the materiality, the tangibility) *of things hoped for*. Now that tells me something very important about hope. Hope by itself has no substance.

Hope Has No Substance

There is nothing about hope that you can see, smell, taste, touch or hear. Because if you could, then you would not need any faith. So faith must be something in order for it to be the substance of things that are hoped for. When I add faith to my hope, then I give my hope substance, materiality, tangibility—something that I can eventually see, smell, taste, hear or touch.

Hope Is a Goalsetter

Hope is a goalsetter. Hope sets the goal, but faith goes and gets it. Now, you must have hope. You cannot live without hope. But if you do not have some way to reach your hope, then your hope will never have anything that you can ever see, smell, taste, hear or touch and that is important.

Here is what hope will do. Number one, hope sets the goal. Number two, hope will keep you alive. That is what kept my wife and me alive for seventeen years—our hope. We had it bad financially. It was a real struggle.

We hoped for a better day, but that hope did not bring the better day. All it did was keep us alive. Here is another thing hope will do. Hope will let you smile while the ship is sinking, but faith will keep the ship afloat. That is a big difference.

What hope does is affect your attitude about the circumstances, but faith will change the circumstances. That is the difference, and it is a major difference.

That is what many Christians are doing—they are just hoping. "Well, I hope God is going to heal me." He is not. Do not worry about it. You are going to die. Either that, or, you may recover, depending on the severity of the condition, or if you have a good doctor or surgeon. But if you say, "I'm hoping God's going to do it," forget it. It will never happen, because that is not faith. God is a faith God.

Hope is like a dream. Have you ever dreamed? Your dream, at the time you were dreaming it, was more real than reality. In fact, you thought it was reality. And perhaps your spouse even told you after you woke up how you were acting while you were dreaming, making noise and sounds of all kinds.

Maybe you were dreaming about going to Mars and you were just about to land on the planet. Or maybe you were dreaming about breaking the 100 meter record in the Olympic games. Or maybe you were flying the fastest airplane and you were going to attain the fastest speed any human had ever flown before, and you were right there. I mean it was so clear, you could taste it.

It was so good, and just at the time you were about to reach out and realize the fulfillment of your dream, just about the time it was to come into focus, into manifestation, suddenly, the telephone rings, and you reach over and grab the phone, "Hello, hello." And it was the wrong number. You hung it up and tried to go back to your dream, but poof, your dream was gone! Has that ever happened to you?

The reason that the dream went *poof* was because dreams have no substance, and that is exactly what hope is. If you do not have any faith to go with your hope, your hope is like a dream. It can never, ever come to pass. Like I say, it will keep you alive. It will let you smile while they are repossessing your car and foreclosing on your house.

It will let you smile while the marshal is pulling all of your goodies out of the house and you are standing there with your kids crying, wondering where you are going to go. It will give you a good attitude, but it will never change your circumstances.

Hope Plus Faith Equals Success

But, if you take your faith and add it to your hope, you will keep the ship afloat and you will keep the economic wolf off of your front porch.

The third thing you need to know is, **...faith is...the evidence of things not seen.** Faith is the evidence of things not what? *Seen.* What is evidence? The best definition of evidence that I know of is proof. Can you agree with that?

Let me ask another question. What is proof? What is the purpose of evidence or proof? Let me give you a definition and see if you can go along with this. Evidence or proof validates, substantiates, or proves the existence of something you do not presently have, because if you had it, you would not need any proof of it.

Let me say it this way. Evidence or proof takes the place of the thing that it is the evidence or proof of, until the thing arrives on the scene. Once it arrives on the scene, you do not need any more evidence or proof.

Let me illustrate. Let us say that you are out on an archaeological expedition, and your purpose is to find dinosaur bones. You have been informed that there is a certain area that is abounding in fossil remains and you are particularly interested in finding the fossil remains or the bones of a Tyrannosaurs Rex.

Everyone has a pick ax and you begin digging in this hillside. After a while, someone puts his ax into the ground and you hear something go, *thud*. It is not dirt. He hit something solid. He puts his pick ax down, takes some smaller tools and a little brush, and very gingerly--because he does not want to destroy anything--starts moving the dirt. He takes a flashlight, looks in that hole, and sees something white. It looks like a bone.

Everyone converges on that particular spot on the mountainside and you begin to very gingerly take the dirt away. Finally, embedded in the side of the mountain you see the skeletal remains of Tyrannosaurus Rex. This is one of the finest specimens you have ever found. A beautiful skeleton, totally intact, of a Tyrannosaurus Rex. You are all gloating about it, and patting one another on the back.

What do you have? You have proof or evidence of the existence of Tyrannosaurus Rex. But you do not have Tyrannosaurus Rex, you only have proof of Tyrannosaurus Rex's existence.

While you are standing there, looking at these bones, suddenly the ground begins to shake. Then you hear these huge footsteps, and up over the hill comes Tyrannosaurus Rex. We do not need any more evidence or proof. We have Tyrannosaurus Rex. The bones (evidence/proof) took the place of the dinosaur, until the dinosaur arrived. Therefore, proof or evidence is temporary, until such time as what the proof, or evidence is of, arrives on the scene.

Again, it says **...faith is...the evidence** (or proof) **of things not seen.** Faith itself is the proof. Faith is the evidence of things not seen.

Seen Means Perceived by the Senses

What is the first thing that comes into your mind when you hear or see the word *seen*? Eyes. Can you agree with that? Eyes have to do with visual perception. Eyes are receptors or sensory mechanisms that are a part of your anatomy which feeds information to your brain visually.

I submit to you that this word *seen* is not referring to eyes. There is a deeper, spiritual meaning than eyes. Simply because, if you limit this to eyes or visual perception, then you would be cheating yourself out of four-fifths of your body's ability to feed information to you about the universe around you.

There are some things that you can see, but you cannot hear, and there are some things that you can hear that you cannot taste, and there are some things that you can taste that you cannot hear, and there are some things that you can hear that you cannot see, and there are some things that you can see that you cannot touch.

If you limit it just to eyes or visual perception, then you miss out on everything that you can hear, smell, taste or touch. I can see the sun, but I cannot touch it. Right? So, I submit to you that the Holy Spirit is not talking about eyes. There is a better word for *seen*.

Let me give you the Frederick K.C. Price paraphrase version. Instead of saying that "faith is the evidence or proof of things not seen," say, "faith is the evidence or proof of things not *perceived by your senses*."

This is a bomb. And here is where many people are missing it with faith. If faith is the evidence or proof of things not perceived by your senses, then that means in order to walk by faith, you have to leave the realm of the senses, and that is utterly frightening to humans. Why? Because every single thing that you have ever learned, you have learned through your senses. When you talk about leaving your senses, it is the most frightening thing in the world, because now you are out there with nothing to hold on to that is tangible.

If you were to take a man, blow his ears out so he cannot hear, destroy his sense of smell, put both of his eyes out, rip out his tongue so he could not taste anything and cut off all of his ability to touch anything, there is no way that he could learn anything about the universe around him, because you have destroyed all of his ability to perceive the universe.

To walk by faith, you will have to leave the realm of the senses. You cannot walk by faith and look at your senses to find out where you are with God. You have to walk by faith, not by your senses. And that can be a frightening thing, because sometimes your senses are telling you one thing and faith is telling you something else.

Think about this. You are driving down the highway on a summer day, and way down the highway it looks like you are going to run into some water. But there is no water. It is called a *mirage* or heat wave. But it looks like water, does it not? That is how your senses can fool you.

How about this. On a nice hot summer night when the moon is full, it can come up off of the horizon like a huge orange ball, gigantic in size. That is about six or seven o'clock in the evening. You go out about one o'clock in the morning, that very same moon is straight up in the sky, and it is blue/white and only about one-tenth of the size it was when you saw it at the horizon. It is no longer orange in color. Did the moon change or do we have two moons? No. It is the same moon, but it is a matter of perspective that makes it look different.

The sense of sight is affected by the perspective. Since faith is, in fact, the evidence or proof of things not perceived by the senses, then there must be another world. A world that is outside and beyond this three-dimensional, physical world, a world that can only be entered into by faith. And there is. It is called the world or realm of God. It is the spirit world. And it is more real than this three-dimensional, physical world.

The only way you get into that world is with your faith. For instance, if you want to pick up an FM broadcast on a radio, you have to flip the button to FM. You cannot flip in to AM because AM and FM are different wave links.

If you want to pick up anything on the FM band, you

have to have an FM radio which is technically a receiver. It does not send anything. All it does is receive signals from the transmitter. But you have to have an FM radio. If you try to pick up FM on an AM radio, it will not work. If you try to pick up God on your senses, it will not work. You have to pick up God on *"FM"* which is *"faith."*

If you want to pick up things in the sense realm, you have to do it through *"AM"* which is your *"body."* If you ever try to mix the two, you will be in trouble. That is where many Christians are missing it. They are trying to pick up God on the AM band, and God is on the FM band, on the F-A-I-T-H band. And if you do not have faith operating, you are not going to pick up God.

13

Faith Is the Evidence of the Unseen

Faith is the proof of things not perceived by the senses. Let me ask you a question. How can you have proof of something that is nonexistent? You cannot. How can you have proof of an apple if there is no such thing as an apple? It is an impossibility.

Therefore—and here is an incredible truth—if God says that faith is the evidence or proof of things not perceived by the senses, then there must be some things that exist that are outside the realm of the senses. Things that can only be contacted with your faith, and faith becomes the proof or the evidence of them, until they are physically manifested in your life.

How am I going to find out what is out there in that spirit world? How will I know that a picture of an elephant is in fact the proof of the existence of an elephant if I have never seen an elephant? How does a child know what is an apple or an orange? Because a parent told the child that is an apple or an orange. You could tell the child that the orange is the apple and the apple is the orange and that a pear is a banana and that is what the child will think.

We Know the Spirit World by the Bible

The only reason we know what we know is because someone told us so. Well, God (our heavenly Parent) has told us what is in the spirit world. He put it all in the Bible.

That is why the Bible is so important. That is why Satan has so cleverly kept the Bible out of most churches and out of most preaching and teaching. Because this book will tell you what is in the spirit world, in God's realm.

Faith is the evidence or the proof of things that are not perceived by the senses. So, in order to walk by faith, I have to leave the realm of the senses. But how am I going to know what is out there if I cannot see it, smell it, taste it, touch it, or hear it? I have to go by God's Word.

God's Word tells me what is out there in that spirit world. God's Word tells me what an elephant looks like in the spirit world. God's Word tells me what a boat looks like in the spirit world. So I have to become an astute, understanding person about God's Word, because if I want to know what is in the realm of God, I have to know the Word of God.

I like to think of God's Word as a guide to tell me what is out there. For instance, if I wanted to look at television tonight at 7:30 and I did not know what is on channel whatever, I would get a television guide. I would not guess about it and I would not waste any time. I would get a television guide. I would look under the day and time to find out what was playing. I do not have to guess. All I have to do is look it up in the TV Guide.

God's TV Guide

God has given us a TV Guide, so to speak. God is transmitting from His great transmitter in heaven twenty-four hours a day. The signal is coming in loud and strong. If I want to know what is playing on God's TV, all I have to do is get a TV Guide, which is really an inventory list of what is being aired. If I need a little healing, I would just flip over to channel First Peter 2:24 and find out that what is playing tonight is, **By whose stripes you were healed.**

If I have a need for things, I would flip over to Philippians Channel (chapter) 4:19 to find out what is playing. It says, **My God shall supply all your need.** If I have a temptation with fear and think that fear is going to come in and overwhelm me, I just flip over to (channel) Second Timothy 1:7 and I find out that **God has not given us a spirit of fear, but of power and of love and of a sound mind** is playing.

The Bible becomes my TV Guide to tell me what is being transmitted on God's great transmitter.

Faith is the evidence or the proof of things that are not perceived by the senses. So I have to walk outside the realm of the senses. I cannot rely on my senses. "Well, I don't feel anything." You are not supposed to.

If you judge anything on how you feel, you have already missed it. And that is what most people do. They say, "Well, I can't feel anything. How do I know I have something and I can't feel it? I can't feel it and I can't see it. How do I know that I have it?" God said so. "But how do I know God is there?"

We Know God Through the Evidence of Faith

How do you know He is *not* there? There is equal evidence. In fact, there is really more evidence to support the existence of God than there is to deny His existence, if you really think about it. Just use your head for something else other than something to knock on the door with.

Imagine you were walking down the street and you saw a watch on the ground. You did not know what it was, so you picked it up, turned it over, looked at it and then discovered that it was a watch—an item that tells you the time.

Do you think that watch just happened by chance? You take the back off and see all those little wheels turning and interacting with one another. Would you think that came by chance? It speaks to the issue of a maker.

Do you think that just by chance this planet earth makes a circle around the sun every 365 and one-quarter days a year? Think about it. It has never been in for an overhaul, never had the spark plugs changed, never had an oil change, never had to change the tires on it. Can you imagine that being something that would happen by chance? Do you think that you, *physical you*, are a product of mindless chance?

As intricate as the brain, eyes, ears, limbs, internal organs are, do you really believe they are a chance happening? That is about as intelligent as believing that three monkeys could drive a dump truck up to the top of 25,000 foot Mount Everest and back the truck up over to the edge loaded with all kinds of building materials—pipe, wires, plaster, dry wall, wood, nails, bolts, plumbing fixtures, toilets, etc.

One monkey pulls the lever, the truck goes up, all these materials fall out and fall 25,000 feet straight down to the bottom of the mountain. By the time they get to the bottom, they form a complete three bedroom house with wallpaper on the walls and carpet on the floors!

There is more evidence to substantiate a Creator than there is to deny a Creator. God has revealed Himself in His Word. Jesus said in John 4:24 talking to the woman at Jacob's well outside the city at Sycar in Samaria, that **God is Spirit**.

God is not a man. He is not flesh and blood. He is a Spirit. And actually, so are we. But you need a physical body-suit to exist in this three-dimensional physical world, because you were created for this world. That is why fish can swim in the water and live. They were made for the water. You take a fish out of water, and he will suffocate and die.

Put a man in water and he will suffocate and die. You call it drowning. But it is really suffocation. You suffocate because you cannot breathe air through water. Fish cannot breathe air through air. Fish breathe air through water. Man breathes air through air. Man cannot breathe air through water. So fish have to have a gill system to live under water.

Man Is a Spirit

Man has to have a body-suit to live in this three-dimensional world. But at your heart, at the real center and core of you, you are a spirit made in the image and likeness of God. God is a Spirit. If you are made in His image and likeness, you must be like God.

The way you have to contact or relate to God is by faith. It is amazing how you can see this in what you call, other kinds of disciplines, such as music, but when it comes to the things of God, all of a sudden it becomes esoteric. All of a sudden it becomes twilight zone time.

You cannot take a piece of sheet music and write alphabets on the charts. If you look at sheet music, music has notes. This is the language of music. And you have to know the notes if you are going to play it according to the music.

When it comes to writing or reading, you have to use the alphabet. You cannot use notes. You cannot write letters with notes, but you have to write music with notes because notes are the language of music. The alphabet is the language of speaking and writing.

Faith is the language of the Kingdom of God. If you do not know the language of musical notes, you will be at a great disadvantage when it comes to reading, writing or playing music. It is the same thing when it comes to reading and writing without knowing the alphabet.

You Must Know the Language of Faith

If you do not know the language of faith, you are not going to be able to function in the Kingdom of God. You will be just like many people who do not know music. They can go to the musical instruments and make a lot of noise. But that is all it is, noise. It is not harmony; it is not symphony; it is not melody; it is just plain noise.

That is the way it is with many people in the Kingdom of God. They are making a lot of noise, but they are not operating by faith, and that is why things are not working for them.

Get Out of the Sense Realm

The more you get out of the sense realm and into the spirit realm, the easier it will be to walk by faith. As you walk by faith, it becomes a conditioning process. I have been doing this for over twenty-five years, faithfully. So I do not need to *see* anything. I do not need to *feel* anything. I just take God at His Word. I am not moved by what I see. I am only moved by what I believe. And I believe the Word of God.

This is why I do not have any problems with faith. I just made a choice to do that. And you can do the same thing. I am not anyone special. I do not have anything special. I just made a choice that I was going to walk by faith and not by sight, that I was going to walk in victory. I found out that God honors His Word. But I have to *know* the Word and I have to *operate* based on that Word in order to put God's power into operation.

Did you know that there were 747 jumbo jets parked right outside the Garden of Eden? There were Concord jetliners that fly 1300 miles an hour parked right next to the

747 jumbo jets? They had AM/FM radios in the garden. They had UHF/VHF television. They had satellites and satellite communication. They had radar. It was right there in the garden. They had electric lights. You did not know there were electric lights in the Garden of Eden? Absolutely.

If you stop and think about it, man has created nothing. Man did not create flying. Birds were doing that before man ever came along. All man did was to find out how to cooperate with the existing laws—laws that God set in motion before He put Adam and Eve in the garden.

Electricity was already there. All man did was discover how to cooperate with the law so that it would produce good for us instead of frying us! Even though electricity can light your house, it can also kill you. None of these things were created by man. Man just discovered how to cooperate with the laws.

When Orville and Wilbur Wright made their first flight at Kittyhawk, they did not invent flying. They just found out how to cooperate with the laws of aerodynamics. But that information was already there in the Garden of Eden. Do you understand what I'm saying?

Just as you have to learn how to cooperate with the laws of aerodynamics in order to fly, so God has laws that govern the spirit world. Those laws are activated by faith. That is why faith is so important, and why the devil fights the message of faith so much. He does not want you to find out how to operate in the laws and begin to receive the benefits of the Kingdom of God.

Romans 10:8:

> **But what does it say? "The word is near you, in your mouth and in your heart" (that is, the word of faith which we preach).**

Paul was preaching, *the faith message* 2,000 years ago.

What does he mean, **The word is near you, in your mouth**? What is it in your mouth for? *To speak it out.* Then he says, **...and** (also) **in your heart.** What is it in your heart for? *To believe it.*

Your heart is not the blood pump. It's the center of your three-fold nature. When the Bible says *heart,* it means the spirit of man, using the word metaphorically, because it means the center and the core of your three-fold nature.

You are a spirit, you have a soul and you live in a body. You are three parts.

When you say the heart of the problem, what do you mean? You mean the center and core of the problem, and around which everything else revolves. When you say the heart of the melon, what do you mean? The center and core of the melon. That around which everything else revolves.

When you say the heart of the tree, what do you mean? You mean the center and core of the tree. When the Bible says the heart of man, that means the center and core of man. What is man? He is a spirit, he has a soul and he lives inside of a body.

You cannot believe God with your mind. This is where many intellectuals have a challenge with faith, because they are so accustomed and conditioned to evaluating everything and calculating everything with their human intellect. There is nothing wrong with human intellect in its right place. But when it comes to the things of God, you cannot walk by your intellect—you have to walk by faith.

The Word of Faith

Look at verse 8 again:

> But what does it say? "The word is near you, in your mouth and in your heart" (that is, the word of faith which we preach).

What should preachers preach? The word of faith! When we preach the word of faith, what do we preach? The Gospel! And when we preach the Gospel, what do we preach? Good news!

What happens when you get news? You get information. Once you have information you become the possessor of what? Knowledge. Notice the progression: Word of faith which we preach; Gospel, or good news; news imparts information; and information brings you knowledge. But what kind of information and what kind of knowledge? Information and knowledge about God. So he says,

> **What does it say? "The word is near you, in your mouth and in your heart" (that is, the word of faith....**

Word of faith! Now he calls it the **word of faith.** That is interesting. Why not just say the Word of God, because it *is* the Word of God? Why does he call it the word of faith? He calls it the word of faith because of Romans 10:17:

> **So then faith comes by hearing, and hearing by the word of God.**

Faith Is God's Modus Operandi

Now this is God's M.O.—His modus operandi, or mode of operation. Faith comes by what you hear. You will get no faith by reading the Bible. "Well, Brother Price, are you saying I shouldn't read the Bible?" I did not say that.

The Bible says you are to be diligent to present yourself to God, a worker who does not need to be ashamed, rightly dividing the word of truth. (2 Tim. 2:15.) It does not say anything about presenting yourself to get any faith.

Faith only comes by what you hear. What you get when you study the Bible is revelation knowledge. God has designed the system to work this way. Faith comes by hearing. That is why it is so important what you hear. Because whatever enters in through the ear gate is going to affect your faith either positively or negatively.

That is the reason why so many Christians do not have any active faith going for them, because they go to churches where they are not hearing the Word of God. They are hearing *about* the Word of God. They are hearing *about* God, but they are not really hearing from God based on His Word. Faith comes. If faith comes, it must have come from somewhere, and it must not have been there before it came there or it would not have come there—it would already be there. Faith comes by hearing.

Faith Is Always Present Tense

Notice what it does not say. It does not say, "So then faith comes by *having heard*." "I heard that." "Oh, I heard that last year." "Oh, I don't need to hear that; I heard that." No, no, no! It does not say that faith comes by having heard. That would be past tense. That would mean that you would only have to hear it one time.

It does not say that. It says, **faith comes by hearing**. And the word *hearing* is present tense continuum ad infinitum. What does that mean? It goes into infinity and never stops. It goes on and on and on and on.

Faith comes by hearing. That is why you have to keep hearing it all the time. And every time you hear it, it will stimulate your faith. Now watch this. It says that faith comes by hearing, and hearing by the Word of God. Therefore, faith and the Word of God are synonymous terms. They basically mean the same thing. You cannot have one without having the other.

If you have the Word of God proclaimed, you automatically have faith present. If you have faith present, it has to be because the Word of God has been proclaimed.

Faith Cannot Be Separated From the Word

I like to say it this way. Faith and the Word of God go hand in hand, like the wet with the water. You cannot go to a restaurant and ask a waiter or waitress to bring you a glass of water and hold the wet. You could order a hamburger and say, "Hold the onions," but you cannot order a glass of water and say, "Hold the wet." If you get the water, you get the wet, because wet goes with water. And so does faith go with the proclaimed Word of God.

That is why it is so important what you hear. Faith comes by hearing, and hearing by the Word of God. Now, with that in mind, faith and the Word of God being synonymous, you can interchange them. Let us go back to Hebrews and I will give you the Frederick K.C. Price paraphrase version of Hebrews 11:1 and see if this registers with your spirit. First I will present it as it is written and then I will give you the Frederick K.C. Price paraphrase edition.

Hebrews 11:1:

Now faith is the substance of things hoped for, the evidence of things not seen.

Now I want to read it in the light of Romans 10:17:

So then faith comes by hearing, and hearing by the word of God.

Hebrews 11:1 (author paraphrase):

Now the Word of God is the substance, tangibility or materiality of things hoped for. The Word of God is the proof or evidence of things not perceived by the senses.

Can you see that? That is why knowledge of this Bible is so important. The Bible is my proof. The Bible is my evidence.

How do I know I am healed? Because God—the Bible—says so. The Bible says it is impossible for God to lie. If it is impossible for God to lie, then it must only be possible for God to tell the truth. So if God says I am healed, then I must be healed. "Yeah, but I don't feel like it." Remember, faith is the evidence, *not* how you *feel*.

We have to guard what we hear, because it will affect our faith positively or negatively. Faith comes by hearing. We need to be sure we are hearing what God says.

False Beliefs Come From Hearing Error

Satan has very cleverly infiltrated into the Church years and years ago in the area of music, for instance. He has inspired a lot of songs to be written that are completely worthless in reference to the Word of God. Many are really anti-Word songs without most people realizing it. It is not a matter of anyone's sincerity in writing a song. But you have to be careful what you listen to, because whatever you hear is going to affect your faith.

Some of the things that you think about people, from an ethnic point of view, are the result of what you heard in your home from your parents. You may have never met certain ethnic people. You may have never had any personal contact with them in your life, and yet you may have a very definite opinion about people of other races or cultural backgrounds.

You formed those ideas by what you heard. You have a lot of faith for those ideas because of what you heard. Take our TV ministry for example. The constituency of our television audience is basically Caucasian, or white. (Please do not be offended by this. That is not my intention, but I use this only as an example.)

Most of our support comes from white people. But they will not come to this church, because this church is in the ghetto. They do not want to go to the ghetto because "those niggers are going to steal everything you have because that is their nature—to steal. Black folk are going to steal. You do not want to park your nice car down in the ghetto, because those niggers are going to steal it."

I know it sounds crass, but let us be real. This is the way people talk. You know it and I know it, and you may have never in your life been in close proximity to a black person. But you have been hearing things all your life about black people. "They're not clean. They don't take baths. They smell and they steal."

All I am trying to say is that many people have these ideas, and most of them came because of what they have heard. We have a lot of faith for a lot of negative things because we have heard it all our lives. We never thought there was anything, relative to our faith, based on what we heard and we have been repeatedly saying those things.

Every time you say it, you are hearing it, and you are reinforcing your faith for it without realizing it. Unconsciously, you are developing a negative faith. We have to be careful about what we hear because it is going to affect our faith. If you are not hearing the right thing, you will have a negative faith and you will not have the kind of faith you need to believe for the things in the Kingdom of God.

14

Unscriptural Songs Weaken Faith

I want to give you an illustration so that you do not think I am out to knock people's songs. That is not my purpose, but I am concerned, because what you hear is going to affect your faith. If you look at songs closely, you will find that many songs are designed to rhyme, to fit like poetry. It goes better with the music.

Sometimes the thought is never considered, "Is this in line with the Word of God—does this make sense scripturally?" We go right on singing these songs without thinking. Some songs have become deified. In other words, we exalt the song to a status equal with Jesus. And when you start tampering with the song, you are tampering with a sacred cow. But I believe in killing cows if they need to be killed.

I want to give you one illustration, and you check this out for yourself. I want to give you the verses in a song and then I am going to give you Scripture to compare the verses with as an illustration of the kinds of things that I am talking about. We are going to look at a hymn from a church hymnal.

You Can Be Sincerely Wrong

The person's name who wrote this song originally is at the top of this stanza that we are going to look at. I am not going to mention the name of the person, because I am not trying to put that person down. I have never met the person and I have no quarrel with that person. I am not even

151

questioning their sincerity. All I am questioning is, "Does this song square up with God's Word?"

The name of this song is, *Pass Me Not*. Now again, I am only using this to show you the importance of "faith comes by hearing," and it is going to shock you. I know this may be your favorite song: "Pass me not, O gentle Savior. Hear my humble cry."

If you are not careful, you will get personal about this and think I am attacking you. But I am not! I am only dealing with a principle. But watch this closely and you will see what I am talking about, and then you will become very selective about your music. Because whatever you listen to is going to affect your faith. *Faith comes by hearing*.

Now look at the first verse: "Pass me not, O gentle Savior." *Pass me not*.... The implication is that there is a possibility that the Lord might pass you by. If there were no possibility of the Lord passing you by, then why would you insult Him by saying,"Do not pass me by"? What does *pass me not* mean? Do not pass me by! Is that right? Now we will look at how unscriptural that is.

Hebrews 13:5:

> **Let your conduct be without covetousness; be content with such things as you have. For He Himself has said....**

He Himself has said. He already said it. He is not *going to say it.*

> **...I will never leave you nor forsake you.**

This was written before the song was written. Now, can you not see a conflict between "Pass me not, O gentle Savior," and ...**I will never leave you nor forsake you**?

When I say, "Pass me not," it is like saying that God is a liar and that His Word is unreliable. I cannot trust His Word, so I have to say, "Do not pass me by." He already said, ...**I will never leave you.**... If He will never leave me, then how is He going to pass me by? What an insult that is to God.

What it does is build a kind of faith into your spirit of a God Who is passing by.

Matthew 28:19,20:

Go therefore and make disciples of all the nations, baptizing them in the name of the Father and of the Son and of the Holy Spirit, teaching them to observe all things that I have commanded you; and lo, I am with you always, even to the end of the age.

He did not say, "Lo, there is a chance I might be with you in good times." No, no, no! He said, **Lo, I am with you always.** Then how dare you say, "Do not pass me by"! Do you see a problem there? The Man said, **Lo, I am with you always.** How much time does *always* cover? In fact, how much time is left out of *always*? None!

If you sing that song for twenty-five years and you have *heard* it for twenty-five years, you will develop a lot of faith for a Savior Who is going to pass you by. And He said, **Lo, I am....** He did not say "Lo, I am *going to be.*" That would be future tense. He said, **Lo, I am....** That is present tense.

Let us look at the rest of that verse. "Pass me not, O gentle Savior. Hear my humble cry." I am asking the Lord to hear me.

1 John 5:14,15:

Now this is the confidence that we have in Him, that if we ask anything according to His will, He hears us. And if we know that He hears us....

What an insult it would be, what a slap in the face to say to Him, "Hear my humble cry." The Man already told you that He heard you, and hears you. Now, for you to say, "Hear my cry," is like saying, maybe He will not.

And if we know that He hears us, whatever we ask, we know that we have the petitions that we have asked of Him.

Can you see what an insult that is, and what a destroyer of your faith it is, to say, "Hear my humble cry"? It is like He is not going to hear. "You be sure to hear me, Lord." If you sing that for twenty-five or thirty years, you get a lot of faith for, "Well, maybe He will not hear me."

Because the very question, the fact that you say, "Hear my humble cry," is to say that there is a possibility He might not hear it. But He said He did. And for me to say, "Hear my cry," is like saying, "You are a liar. Your Word is unreliable. I cannot count on You, so I am going to have to pump You up and prime You and then tell You to hear me."

Verse 14:

Now this is the confidence that we have in Him, that if we ask anything according to His will, He *hears* us.

"Pass me not, O gentle Savior. Hear my humble cry. While on others Thou art calling." "While on others thou art calling?" So He is calling on the other folk, whoever they are. But apparently the person who is saying this is not included in the "while on others Thou art calling."

Are you seeing this? That is amazing? We are acknowledging that He is calling on someone. But He is not calling on us. Because if He were calling on us we would be included in the "others" and would not have to say, "While on others Thou art calling, do not pass me by." Can you see that?

You might say, "Why are you taking so much time with this?" I am telling you, this is subliminal. It is very crucial that you understand this, because this principle is building up in you cumulatively, over a whole lifetime—ten, fifteen, twenty-five years you keep hearing this kind of unbelief and it will affect your faith in a negative way. Faith comes by what you hear.

The song said, "While on others Thou art calling, do not pass me by." The whole idea is wrong because that is not what God tells you to do.

Matthew 11:28:

Come to Me, all you who labor and are heavy laden, and I will give you rest.

He is not saying, "I am coming to you." He is telling you to come to Him. Now if He tells me to come to *Him*, then *Him* must plan to be there when I come to *Him*, and *Him* must want to be bothered with me in order to give me an open invitation to come to Him. He is not saying, "While on others Thou art calling, do not pass me by."

There is no doubt about it. I do not have to wonder. He said, **Come to Me...**, *not* "While on others Thou art calling, do not pass me by." No! He said, **Come to Me....** That is His command to me. He is telling you what to do. He is not calling on anyone, because He does not need anyone in order to be Who He is. We are the ones who have the need. We are the ones who have to do the calling, not God. God does not need us, we need God.

Romans 10:13:

For "whoever calls on the name of the Lord shall be saved."

He is not going to call on you. You have to call on Him. He gave you an invitation. We have to honor the invitation by calling on Him.

Unscriptural Songs Create Negative Faith

If you keep singing this song and hearing this, you will get a lot of faith for a God Who may pass by. "Well, maybe He'll call on me. Somebody's at the door. Is that the Lord? Is the Lord knocking?" No! He said,

For "whoever calls on the name of the Lord...."

Verse two of the song goes,

"Let me at Thy throne of mercy, find a sweet relief.
Kneeling there in deep contrition, help my unbelief."

I am already acknowledging that I am disbelieving. "Let me at a throne of mercy, find a sweet relief." Let us find out what the Scripture says. I am just using this one song, and dissecting it, but there are multitudes of songs like this.

What I am trying to get you to see is that faith comes by hearing, and hearing and hearing and hearing and hearing. It is so important what you hear. It is going to affect your faith. Whether consciously or unconsciously, it is affecting your faith.

Here's another example. You have been out in the yard in the summertime mowing the lawn or cutting some branches off the trees. You have been out there for several hours. You go back in the house, and your skin is a different color. You did not go out there to get a tan. You did not go out there to get red. But you see, those ultraviolet rays are affecting you, because you came in contact with them.

When you come in contact with unbelief, whether you realize it or not, it is going to have an impact on you. That is why it is important what you hear, what you listen to. All right, look at this, "Let me at Thy throne of mercy, find a sweet relief."

Hebrews 4:16:

Let us therefore come boldly to the throne of grace, that we may obtain mercy and find grace to help in time of need.

God is talking to you. For you to say to Him, "Let me at a throne of mercy, find a sweet relief." "Let me find it." "Let me come to the throne." "Let me...."

God has already spoken. How dare we say, "*Let*." It is like He is keeping you from it, or like He would keep you from it. "Let me." "Let me." "Mama, let me go out and play." "Let me at a throne of mercy, find a sweet relief. Kneeling there in deep contrition, help my unbelief."

Verse 3 of this song: "Trusting only in Thy merit, would I seek Thy face. Heal my wounded, broken spirit, save me by Thy grace."

I thought these were saved people singing the song. I thought this was a Christian song for Christians to sing. How in the world is a Christian going to get saved? That is why there are so many Christians who belong to multitudes of churches who have a problem with their salvation. They are never sure because they have been listening to songs like this.

They are not sure, because they have a lot of faith for being *unsure*, by what they have heard all their lives. "Heal my wounded, broken spirit. Save me by Thy grace." I thought you were already saved. I thought you said you were born again.

All of this is unscriptural, because God does not heal spirits. There is not a Scripture in the Bible about healing spirits. God does not say anything in His Word about getting your spirit healed. He does talk about your spirit, but not about getting it healed.

John 3:6:
That which is born of the flesh is flesh, and that which is born of the Spirit is spirit.

God does not heal spirits. God tells you, you must be born again. God is not going to heal your existing spirit. He gives you a new spirit when you are born again.

2 Corinthians 5:17:
Therefore, if anyone is in Christ, he is a new creation....

It does not say anything about healing anything. God does not heal spirits. Besides that, the problem with man is not the need to get a broken spirit healed. Man needs a *new* spirit. All the promises of God that have to do with healing have to do with the physical body. God gives you a new heart or spirit. In the old covenant God talked about this fact.

Ezekiel 11:19:

> **Then I will give them one heart, and I will put a new spirit within them, and take the stony heart out of their flesh, and give them a heart of flesh.**

Meaning, "I am going to put in a heart that is soft towards Me and that comes by being born again.

When you sing a song like, "Heal my wounded, broken spirit," that is unscriptural.

Now, the fourth verse:

"Thou the spring of all my comfort, more than life to me. Whom have I on earth beside Thee, who in heaven but Thee."

That is all right. Are you getting the point of what I am talking about? Faith comes by hearing.

"Pass Me Not" is one of the old hymns of the Church. In the charismatic churches they hardly ever sing hymns; they sing choruses. But even with those choruses, you have to be careful what you sing.

There was a song I used to love to sing. This song is a beautiful song. It went, "Kum Ba Ya, Kum Ba Ya" "Come by here, Lord, come by here. Somebody needs You, Lord, come by here."

It is a beautiful song, but it is totally unscriptural because we have already read the Scripture, **Lo, I am with you always.** Now why would you say, "Come by here?" To say, "Come by here," implies He is not already *by here*. Because if He were already *by here*, why would He have to come by where He already is?

There was another charismatic song which I used to love. This song was called, *Let Me Touch Him*.

"Let me Touch Him, Let me touch Jesus, Let me touch Him as He passes by." The Man said, **Lo, I am with you always.** He did not say, "Lo, I am passing by you." So we have to be careful even with these so-called charismatic songs. A lot of them are full of unbelief. They do them because they rhyme, and sell. They sell multitudes of cassette music tapes and sheet music.

I am not saying that the people who are writing the songs mean anything wrong. They are just trying to make something fit—something melodious. Yet those melodious songs are not always in line with the Word of God.

What You Say and Hear Will Affect Your Faith

You have to be careful what you hear, because it is going to affect your faith. You need to be careful about your songs, who you talk to, what radio programs you listen to. And to show you how quickly it works, you go home in the evening, listen to the news, and the next day you are telling folk about what you heard on the news. You have faith for that. "You know what they're saying? They're saying another storm's coming."

You cannot read the signs of the sky yourself; you are not a meteorologist. But you are going by what you heard. "Oh, we had better get ready; there's another rain storm coming. They said it's going to dump about five inches of rain." And you believe that, because that is what you heard.

We are so accustomed to this that we never think about equating it to spiritual values. But the principle is the same.

That is why many people are afraid of life. People are afraid because they have been hearing this all the time. They have a lot of fear, and that fear came by what they heard.

PART V

FAITH IS THE KEY THAT UNLOCKS ALL DOORS

15
Faith Is a Way of Life

Before moving on to the next segment of our study, I want to capsulize what we have already found out about faith. Remember that faith is *now*. Faith is the substance, the materiality, the tangibility of things hoped for. Faith is the evidence or proof of things not perceived by your senses.

In order to walk by faith, you have to leave the realm of the senses. You have to walk by God's Word, because God's Word when proclaimed causes faith to come, because faith comes by hearing and hearing by the Word of God.

2 Corinthians 4:18:

> **While we do not look at the things which are seen, but at the things which are not seen. For the things which are seen are temporary, but the things which are not seen are eternal.**

Remember, faith is the evidence of things not seen. Here is this word *seen* again. If you are not careful, there will be a temptation to relegate this to the area of visual perception. Again, he is not talking about that at all. He is talking about the same thing that he was talking about in Hebrews 11:1. Notice he says,

> **While we do not look at the things which are seen, but at the things which are not seen. For the things which are seen are temporary, but the things which are not seen are eternal.**

Here is another paraphrase version that I believe will help solidify your understanding of this principle.

Faith Must Be a Way of Life

I travel all over the world ministering the Word of God, and I find that people are the same. White people, black people, people of any other ethnicity are all the same, and they are making the same mistakes in reference to faith.

Some start out in a blaze of glory, espousing the message of faith, and then all of a sudden they stop. They go completely opposite and begin to shoot it down, because they do not really understand it. They did not take time to really hear. They got excited about the things that faith will produce and they have not taken the time to develop their faith, so that it is a way of life and not just a way of *getting things*.

If you make faith a way of life, then the *things* will take care of themselves. If you focus on getting things, it will not be a way of life, and as soon as an obstacle comes, you will be discouraged and be ready to throw up your hands. But I want you to know that faith works, and that God's Word produces results. Here is a good illustration of how people miss it.

I want to give the Frederick K.C. Price paraphrased version of Second Corinthians 4:18:

> While we do not look at the things which are (perceived by the senses), but at the things which are not (perceived by the senses). (For or because) the things which are (perceived by the senses) are temporary (or subject to change), but the things which are not (perceived by the senses) are eternal (or everlasting).

Notice carefully in that verse that two things are brought into juxtaposition to each other. One is something that is called *seen things* and something that is called *unseen things*. Seen, unseen. Say this: *Perceived by the senses. Not perceived by the senses*. Those are opposites. Now watch. He says,

While we do not look at the things which are
(perceived by the senses)....

Many People Get Confused About Faith

Here is where many people get all confused about faith.
They do not listen. They do not hear. Just like some of you.
Some people think that I am saying that we are to deny that
we have pain when we have it, or that we are supposed to
deny that our wallet is empty when it is empty, and that
what faith is saying is, "I'm not afraid. I'm not scared," even
when I am trembling.

That is what some people are thinking, but that is *not*
what I am saying. And that is not what the Bible says. So
they have this denial syndrome. They deny that they are
sick. They deny that they do not have enough money. That
is not what the Bible is saying. That is not what faith says.

Faith does not say you do not have pain. Faith does not
say you do not have a tumor. Faith does not say you do not
have an empty wallet. That is not what faith is saying at all.
If you would just read, you would get it.

While we do not look at the things which are seen....

That tells you that the things which are seen must exist,
right? If they did not exist you could not look at them
anyway, because you cannot see something that does not
exist. And God would not tell you not to look at what is not
there. The very fact that He says, **while we do not look at
the things which are seen,** means that the things which are
seen do exist. They are there. The pain is there. The tumor is
there. The empty wallet is there. The empty bank account is
there. The fear is there.

Faith Does Not Look at the Circumstances

Faith is not saying that it is not there, but *faith does not
look at it.* It does not deny it, it just does not look at it and it
does not allow it (the *things seen*) to dictate the terms of our
existence. He is telling you,

While we do not look at the things which are seen, but at the things which are not seen....

What is it that is not seen? *With Jesus' stripes I was healed.* That is what is not seen. What do I look at? I look at, **my God shall supply all [my] need according to His riches in glory by Christ Jesus.** What do I look at? I look at the fact that I have not been given **a spirit of fear, but of power and of love and of a sound mind.**

That is what I look at, and that is what I confess with my mouth. And while I am looking at the things that are not seen by the senses, while I am confessing that, it is causing my faith to generate God's power to such an extent, that it overcomes that which is seen in the natural and wipes it out.

Do Not Deny the Problem

We do not deny the sickness. What we deny is its authority to dictate the terms of our existence. Do you understand the difference? God is not telling us to deny what the senses are telling us. What God is telling you to do is look at the things which are not seen, or not perceived by the senses.

How do you look at something that is not seen? You look at it with the eye of faith. Why? Because faith is the proof of the things not seen. And what is faith? Faith is synonymous with the Word of God. So what does God say?

1 Peter 2:24:
...by whose stripes you were healed.

If you are not healed, then God is a liar. If your needs are not met, God is a liar, because He says in His Word, **My God shall supply all your need**—not the biggest portion of your needs, not the major things; not according to your empty wallet, not according to your bankrupt bank account, but according to His riches in glory by Christ Jesus.

166

I look at what the Word says. The devil has so cleverly kept this Word out of the average denominational church, because if you do not have the Word, you will not have any faith. And if you do not have the Word, you will not know what God's remedies are for the issues of life. Therefore, you will have no other choice but to gravitate to what you see.

That is what most Christians do—they confess what they see. They confess what they feel. "I'm sick. I'm sick. I ain't got no money. I'm just so poor I don't know what I'm going to do." And they think they are being honest.

I used to do it. I used to be a past master at organ recitals. I used to give regular weekly organ recitals. You know, my eye hurts, my ear hurts, my heart hurts, my stomach.... You know, organs. Always whining. Always complaining. "I ain't got no money. I don't know what I'm going to do."

I used to whine and cry so much that I was ashamed of my own whining and crying. But I did not know anything else to do. My church told me, "Hold on. Hang in there. Keep a stiff upper lip. The Lord knows how much you can bear." But I could not go to the creditors with "the Lord knows how much you can bear." They wanted green stuff, and a *lot* of it, and they wanted it *now*. And I did not have it. So, I learned that I have to say what God says.

God Is Not a Liar

God is not a liar. The Bible says that it is **impossible for God to lie**. If God cannot lie, the only alternative is: He must tell the truth. So if God says I am healed, I must be healed.

Do not misunderstand me. We get attacked with sickness and disease and sometimes we have to use natural means to deal with the symptoms, but we will need the power of God to eradicate the cause. Remember, pain is symptomatic. Pain is an effect, it is not the cause. All you have to do to get rid of the pain, is get rid of the cause. If you get rid of the cause, the pain will go automatically.

You can take an aspirin but all the aspirin is doing is anesthetizing your conscious awareness of the pain. You have not dealt with cause yet. Sometimes under certain conditions you will need something to anesthetize you, or you will not be able to keep your mind straight, because of the pain. Pain can be so severe it can render you unable to function.

We may need some natural help, but do not think that the aspirin is curing anything. We still need the power of God, especially with all of these ailments the doctors are coming up with now. They do not have any cures for them. AIDS, for instance, and cancer.

You had better learn how to believe God. They can cut out and cut off, but there are only so many organs and limbs that you can cut off. Let me say it again, we had better learn how to believe God.

2 Corinthians 5:7:
For we walk by faith, not by sight.

Read it again, out loud. You should have sensed something happening to you, on the inside, when you said that, because you heard it. **Faith comes by hearing**. If there is anyone's words you ought to believe, it is your own words. **Faith comes by hearing**.

The Bible did not say *who* you have to hear it from. You can hear it from your own mouth. That is the reason why I am always making positive confessions in line with God's Word. And because I do, people who are ignorant of the Word of God do not understand it and they call me a braggart. "There he goes bragging again."

What they do not understand is, I am not bragging. What I am doing is saying the Word, because every time I say the Word, I hear the Word and I know that my word is good.

Some people cannot be counted on, because their word is not good. They might do what they say they are going to do and they might not. I know what I am going to do because I am determined to do it. My word is good. I would rather die than break my word. That is how much my word means to me.

I have no idea what your word means to you. So that is why I am always saying things. You have to say it. **Faith comes by hearing**. Maybe that is why I have what I have, because I talk it. That is why I am in divine health, because I talk divine health. The Bible says, **...by whose stripes you were healed**. That means I *was* healed. If I *was*, I *am*. If I *am*, I *"is."* And now faith *is*. That is not good English, but I will use anything I can that is not nailed down to get the point across.

He says, **...by whose stripes you were healed**. *Were* is past tense. If you were, you are. And if you are, you *"is."* And Hebrews 11:1 says, **Now faith is. ...by whose stripes you were healed**. *Were* is past tense, indicative of the fact that the time of the action has already taken place.

It is not taking place; it is not going to take place in the future; it has already taken place. It is a done deal as far as God is concerned. It is signed, sealed and delivered. But I have to *know it*. I have to *believe it* and I have to *confess it*, so that what was done, becomes mine personally.

Satan is going to challenge you every step of the way, to see to it that you do not get the benefit. That is where the warfare comes in. That is why we are called upon to fight the good fight of faith, because the devil is not going to back down. He is going to challenge you every step of the way. He will contest every inch of ground. He does not want you to win.

Faith Looks Beyond the Circumstances

You have to stand by faith. You have to say what God says, because God is not a liar. The Bible says, **And my God shall supply all your need...** (Phil. 4:19). So my confession is, "I believe that all my needs are met."

People do not know me. They are only seeing a partially finished product. But you see, I said that more than twenty-five years ago, "I believe that all my needs are met," just as loudly, just as boldly, as I am saying it now and did not have a pot to cook in.

Let me give you an example. We bought a beautiful brand new Chevrolet Caprice one year. I forget what year it was. It was a hardtop convertible with a black vinyl top and white body. It was a beautiful looking car. I like things nice and I like to keep things nice.

My wife put dents on it and dinged it on both sides and the back. I was teaching my daughter, Angela, how to drive, and she decided the way you stop a car is to run into the back of another car, and that guarantees you are going to stop! That car was dented on the front, on the back and on both sides.

I would drive that car all over Southern California ministering. In the early days the Lord opened many doors for me to minister the Word of faith. Then I was just as bold as I am now, just as bold as a lion. I was saying, "My God shall supply all my need." "Every one of my needs are met according to His riches in glory by Christ Jesus." "I am healed from the top of my head to the soles of my feet." "I am an overcomer." "I am the head and not the tail." "I am blessed going out and coming in."

My dear, darling wife was sitting in the congregation almost in fear—natural fear—thinking that someone might go out of that building and see that dinged up car that I was driving. She was embarrassed. She was saying, "They're going to think he's crazy, talking about all his needs are met, and then look at that car all banged up."

I was seeing beyond that car. I was not looking with the eyes of the cranial cavity. I was looking with the eye of faith. It did not matter to me what anyone thought. If you are going to walk victoriously, you cannot be concerned about what people say. You cannot be concerned about what they are going to think, because they are going to think what they want to think.

You have to go with the Word. You have to walk the Word, teach the Word, preach the Word, talk the Word, believe the Word and act on the Word. I was making my confession. I was putting faith into operation. **For we walk by faith, not by sight** (2 Cor. 5:7).

Remember that faith is synonymous with what? The Word of God. So we could simply read it like this: *For we walk by the Word and not by the senses*. Well, how am I going to walk by something I do not know? That is why the devil has kept the Book out of most churches. If the people do not have the Word, what else can they go on, but what they see in the natural? That can be dangerous to your well-being.

John 14:30:

> **I will no longer talk much with you, for the ruler of this world is coming, and he has nothing in Me.**

Jesus called Satan the *ruler* of this world.

In Second Corinthians 4:4, Paul calls Satan **...the god of this age....** In other words, Satan is the god of the sense realm. That is why he promotes so much emotionalism in the churches around the world. If he can keep your attention and keep you occupied by what you feel and what you see in the sense realm, he will hook a ring in your nose, attach a chain to it and lead you around for the rest of your life, because he is the god of the sense realm.

But God the Father wants you to walk by faith, because He is the God of the spirit realm. And when you walk by the Word, when you walk by faith, then you lock the devil out.

Satan Is the God of the Sense Realm

As long as you walk by your senses, you are, without realizing it, allowing Satan to dictate the terms of your existence, because he is the god of this world, which means the god of the sense realm. That is why it says, **For we walk by faith, not by sight**. We walk by the Word and not by the senses.

You do not deny the senses. When it is cold, you are cold. When it is hot, you are hot. If they stick you with a pin, it hurts. You do not deny the senses. You just do not *look* at them. We do not allow those things to tell us what to do. We let the Word of God tell us what to do. For we walk by the Word, not by the senses.

I have to know the Word in order to walk by it. Now, we could legitimately ask the question, "Why does God tell us to walk by faith?" Because that is the way He has structured the system. It works that way by faith, not by sight. Because sight is unreliable.

16
Ignore the Negative

We know that we are supposed to look at the things which are not seen. We find out what they are by looking at the Word of God. But in the meantime, what are we supposed to do about the things which are seen? He said do not look at them, but they are still there. What do we do about their existence? We ignore them.

Someone says, "How do you do that?" The same way you ignore me when you do not want to be bothered with me. You act like I am not there. You cannot *say* I am not there, because I am. "Ignore" means to act like something is not there, but you do not *say* that it is not there.

Ignore Circumstances Like
You Ignore People

It is amazing how we do not have any problem with that in the natural world. We can ignore people; we can ignore certain kinds of things; we can act like we did not hear someone calling us.

Someone is calling you, and you just keep walking right along. You act just like you do not hear them. That is called ignoring them. You are not saying that they are not there, you are just not allowing them to impact upon your present circumstances.

That is what we do when we do not look at the things which are seen. We do not deny their existence, we simply do not look at them. We ignore them.

Let us, for the sake of discussion, say that you have been diagnosed as having a tumor. *Do not look at it*. God does not say deny its existence; just do not look at it. Do not say it is not there, just do not look at it.

What are you to do with things that exist? With something that exists, number one, ignore it. Number two, say what God says about it. Since God cannot lie, as I have said before, the only alternative is that God must tell the truth. So whatever God says about me, that must be me. Not because I am experiencing it, but because that is what God says about me, and God cannot lie.

It must be true, even though I do not see it, hear it, smell it, taste it or touch it, *yet*! It has to be true, since God cannot lie.

Talk God Talk

One of the things you have to learn early on, if you are to be successful with God, is to learn how to *talk God talk*.

In other words, you must learn how to *think God thoughts* and *talk God talk*.

Let me give you a personal example. I have been the pastor of Crenshaw Christian Center for over twenty years. And in that time I have never been out of my pulpit on Sunday morning for a physical ailment. The only times I have ever been out are when I was on vacation or I was out of the country and could not get back. But I have never not come and preached the Word because of some physical ailment. I am using myself as a guinea pig to make a point.

I have six assistant pastors, and if I was sick and could not make it, all I would have to do is get on the telephone and tell my secretary, "I cannot make Sunday, because I am sick. Assign one of my assistants to take my place." There would be nothing wrong with that. That is normal. But I refuse to do that because the inventory list says that with Jesus' stripes I was healed. So I believe that I am well.

Now, the illustration: *I am telling you to do this* because I am trying to show you from a practical point of view how you are going to have to act if you intend to be victorious in this faith life, over time. I am telling you that these are the kinds of things that have caused me to win.

I had to have a wisdom tooth pulled. The tooth was growing the wrong way, and in the natural, it was a mess. So my decision was to have the tooth pulled out because the doctor said it could damage the rest of the gum system. So I had it pulled out.

My regular dentist was not in town, so I was sent to an alternate dentist. This man did not know me and I did not know him. He was strictly operating from his professional background and strictly from what he saw. He determined that the tooth had to come out. So he extracted the wisdom tooth.

When a tooth comes out, blood from the gums will seep into the cavity and form a protective clot over the exposed nerve. Once the tooth is pulled out, the nerve is exposed. When air or cold hits that nerve, you are going to climb walls because of the pain.

This clot began to form. The dentist gave me some pain pills and told me to take it easy, and that everything would be all right. That was in the middle of the week. I was scheduled to go to church on Sunday.

What he did not tell me was that I had to be very careful if I coughed or spit up. An excessive amount of blood was draining from the cavity and running down my throat, and I spit up not only the excess blood in my throat, but the blood clot that had formed over the cavity. I ended up with what is technically called a dry socket. You have a completely exposed nerve.

When I talked or moved my jaw and the air hit that nerve, I experienced blinding, blue-white throbbing pain. I could not get in touch with my dentist, and I had to come to church. At that time, I was doing two morning services. I came to church. Why? Because God said, **while we do not look at the things which are seen**. He did not say deny them, but do not look at them. Ignore them.

I had two choices—call an assistant pastor or come to church as usual. Understand, at the time, I did not know what was happening to me. All I felt was pain. I felt pain that was so severe, it felt like someone had a jackhammer sitting on top of my head. Three demons had my mouth open and the fourth demon was sticking the jackhammer right down in that dry socket and was turning it on as fast as it would go.

My head felt like seventeen 747 jumbo jets had just exploded. It was so painful, I was almost blinded with the pain. Every movement of my jaw was like sticking an ice-pick in that nerve.

Remember, however, He said, **do not look at the things which are *seen***. So I did not. I looked at what God's Word says. The Word of God says **with Jesus' stripes I was healed**. The Word of God says **Himself took my infirmities and bore my sicknesses**. So I claimed my healing.

I came on to church and preached two services. I talked for two hours straight. Every single word was excruciating, blinding pain, without a second's let up. You see, I believe what I preach. I told you I am not telling you to do this. I am just telling you that this is how the system works.

I believed I was well, so I had to act like I was well. You have to make up your mind and decide whether you want to pay that kind of price or not.

I am not any better than anyone else. I am not due any kind of credit. "Oh, isn't he wonderful?" No, I am just trying to show you how it works. He said do not look at the things which are seen, but look at the things which are not seen. Well, the things which are not seen said I am well, I was healed. So I believed that I was well.

If I actually believe that I am well, then I should be on my job, because well people are on their job. It is only sick people who do not go to work. Since I was not sick, I had to go to work. My work is to go and preach. So I had to act like I was well.

If I had stayed home, I would have been saying that I was sick. And I will not do that. I am not telling you what to do, but I will not do that. I had the pain in the natural, but I was sustained by my spirit by the Holy Spirit, and that was why I could do it.

Not one single person in that congregation, other than my wife, knew that I was in that kind of pain. I could not talk about it, and say, "You all pray for me. Pray for pastor. I'm in such pain." I did not say that. I wanted to say that.

My flesh wanted to say it to the congregation, loud and clear, "Have mercy on me. I'm going through such pain. You have to feel sorry for me. You have to feel sorry for Pastor Price, I'm in such pain. Oh, please come on and give me a little bit of tender loving care and concern. At least get an expression on your faces that says you are empathizing with me." No! I could not do that because I believed I was well. So I had to act like I was well. Here is the Bible principle that supports what I am talking about.

Romans 4:17:

(As it is written, "I have made you a father of many nations") in the presence of Him whom he believed— God, who gives life to the dead and calls those things which do not exist as though they did.

This was Paul talking about faith and using the patriarch Abraham as an illustration of it. God had told Abraham he would have a child. Paul is quoting what was written: **I have made you a father of many nations....**

When God said that to Abraham, he did not have any children. In the natural Sarah could not have any children, but here is Almighty God, a holy God Who cannot lie, saying **I have made you a father of many nations**, and the man did not have any children.

How could God, the Creator of the ends of the earth, a God Who requires man to live in holiness, Who demands us to live righteously, have the audacity to lie to this man Abraham and tell him, "I have made you the father of many nations," and Abraham had no children and could not in the natural have any. We have a dilemma here.

The Bible says God cannot lie, meaning it is impossible for God to lie. Notice what God did not say. He did not say, "I am thinking about making you the father of many nations someday off in the distant future." He did not say, "I have been mulling it over in my mind, Abe, and I am just about ready to make you the father of many nations." He said, *I have*, that means it's already done...He did not say *I am making* you, present tense, He said *I have* made you the father of many nations. Was God lying? No!

Here is why God could say that, and this is what I meant by "*God speak*" and "*God think*." You are going to have to learn how to "*God speak*" and "*God think*," if you are going to be a victorious, overcoming, joyful Christian. You can be a Christian, but not necessarily a victorious Christian. Notice again, the Scripture says,

> **(As it is written, "I have made you a father of many nations") in the presence of Him whom he believed— God, who gives life to the dead and calls those things which do not exist as though they did.**

That is how God operates. God calls those things that do not exist as though they did. "Brother Price, that doesn't make sense." You are absolutely right, because it is not sense; it is faith. Go to the head of the class; you made an "A."

Understand this, faith is faith and sense is sense. Dogs are dogs and hogs are hogs. Hogs are not dogs; dogs are not hogs; faith is not sense and sense is not faith. Faith is faith, and sense is sense, and dogs are dogs and hogs are hogs. You never mix them.

"Well, do you think I am that unintelligent, Dr. Price? Do you think that I am stupid? I want you to know I'm not going to be that dumb and believe something I cannot figure out with my brain." Why not? You do it all the time, Mr. Smart. You are just like everyone else, you believe things all the time and have no actual proof for them. Think about this, you have been going around all the time telling folk you are ninety-nine years old, or thirty-five years old or thirty-seven years old.

You have been telling folks, "That is my mama and that is my daddy and I was born in Jackson, Mississippi," or wherever, and you do not know where you were actually born. You are merely taking someone's word for it. They told you that is where you were born. You do not know for sure. Now all of a sudden, when it comes to God, you have to have scientific proof that these things are so.

You have no proof as to where you were born, you have no proof as to who your mother and father were. All you have is what someone told you. Not only that, but if one of those people who told you that has consistently lied about other things down through the years, how do you know they are not lying about who your mama is and who your daddy is?

"Yes, but how can I call those things that do not exist as though they did? It doesn't make sense!" Again, you are right, it does not make sense, but it makes faith. God calls those things which do not exist as though they did. So God says, "Let the sick say they are well." First Peter 2:24, **...by whose stripes you were healed.** Let the weak say they are strong.

Philippians 4:13:

I can do all things through Christ who strengthens me.

Why? Because they are in Him, if they will believe it and act like it, instead of acting weak and sick.

That is what makes the power work, when you *act* like what God said about you is true. What you want to do, because that is the natural way of doing things in the sense realm, is feel well, then you will tell everyone you are well. When you walk by faith, you have to say, "I believe *I am* well." "I believe *I am* healed."

So, with the tooth situation I believed that I was well, and since I was well, I had to act like it. I had to call those things which did not exist as though they did. I did it by my actions and I did it by my words. As a result I came to church.

That is just one illustration. I have had many other times when I have been in pain but did not tell anyone, because I believed I was well. There have been days when I have walked into church and could hardly move my leg.

The devil was telling me that it was arthritis, but I never accepted it as arthritis. But I could feel the pain. I have walked into church when the big toe on my left foot hurt so bad, it was painful just to set my foot down. It was painful to put the shoe on the foot.

My congregation has never seen me limping and preaching. Now there is nothing wrong with that, if that is what you have to do, but I believed I was well, so I dared to believe that when I put my foot out there and stepped down on it, it was going to support my body, pain or no pain. And I have had manifestation after manifestation of healings *while* I was up acting like what God said about me was true.

You Must Be Personally Convinced Faith Works

I had to act like I was well. So I had to do what? I had to *look not at the things which are seen.* And the pain was seen; it was there. But I acted like I was well. Now understand, you cannot do this or try to do it because Fred does it. The only way you can do this: *you have to be*—not your mama, not your daddy, not your brother, not your sister, not your fiancé, not your wife, not your husband, not your dog or your frog—but *you* have to be absolutely, unequivocally convinced, before this will ever work for you.

Do not do this if you are trying to be like someone else. That is what some have done. They were going to try it and then the pain got too bad—they could not stay with it, so it did not work. It did not work because they got scared. And as soon as fear comes in, faith goes out. In such cases, the best thing to do is get to your doctor as fast as you can.

I am not saying that I do not do something about pain, but it is not always convenient to do something about it at the time. The devil is slick. He will wait until you are in a position where you cannot conveniently do something about it, then he will stick you with something.

Remember, God said, **while we do not look at the things which are seen.** Well, the things which are seen are actually there, but now what do we do about them? All He said was, "Do not look at them." He did not say deny their existence. So what do you do in the meantime? Maybe you have pain, so what do you do?

Unfortunately, some Christians never listen to what I am saying in total. They never really listen. They get the idea that what I am saying is that you are supposed to deny the pain is there. You are supposed to deny that you feel bad. No! No! He simply said, "Do not look at how you feel and what you see." He did not say, "Deny it."

I never talk about how I feel. That is the difference. I do not deny that I am in pain. If you ask me point blank, "Fred, are you in pain?" I only have two choices. Either I am going to say no if I am not in pain, or I will say yes if I am in pain.

What I have learned how to do, is to say what God says. He calls those things which do not exist as though they did. So if it is all right for the Father to call those things which do not exist as though they did, it has to be all right for the children to call those things which do not exist as though they did. And so since the Word says with Jesus' stripes *I was* healed, and if *I was, I am* and if *I am, I "is"* and *now faith is. I am* healed. So, I confess that I believe that I am healed.

Hold on to the Evidence

In the meantime, until the manifestation comes, what do you do? If you already had it, you would not have to believe it. If you already had it, you would not have to use any faith. Remember we found out in Hebrews 11:1, faith is the proof, faith is the evidence. You do not need any evidence if you are already well. The very fact that you are well is your evidence. You only need evidence or proof when you do not physically have it yet.

The Word of God takes the place of what I do not have. It says with Jesus' stripes I was healed, so I have to believe that I am healed. I have to say that. But now, in the meantime, what do you do about that pain, about that blinding pain? Sometimes you are in a position, like I said, where you cannot do anything about it.

Personally, I do not have any problems with medication, doctors, operations, or anything, I have never said that I did. I have always striven, through faith, to rise above that so that I do not have to use it.

I believe in spare tires, but I would rather ride on my four good ones than use the spare. But guess what? If I went out one day and one of the four was flat, do you think I would just sit there and do nothing when I have a perfectly good spare in the trunk? I would pull that spare out and put it on the ground and take that bad one somewhere and get it fixed. But my faith is not in the spare.

There have been times when I had pain and I called my doctor. Understand, I am exposing myself so that you will understand how to do things and not get in bondage, thinking, "Well, I just have to sit here and suffer and be in pain." No, you do not. The reason I did what I did was because I could not get to my dentist. I did not know what to do, because I really did not know what was happening to me. I had never heard the words "dry socket." I did not know what was going on. I could not get to my dentist to find out, or to ask him what to do or so he could give me some medication.

That is why I went on and did what I had to do. Because I believed I was well with or without the medication. I still believed that I was well and I was going to act that way and talk that way.

I am not trying to hide anything from you. There have been times when I had pain in my foot, I called my doctor and he came over and stuck a needle right down in that foot to give me some relief. He has even given me medication in pill form. I do not have a problem with that. That is not taking away the cause, and the doctor will tell you that.

Pain Is a Symptom, Not a Cause

The shot is not going to take away the cause, because if it did, all you would need is just one shot and you would never have that pain again the rest of your life. But the shots and the pills deal only with the symptoms. Pain is not causative; pain is symptomatic. Pain is telling you that something is wrong.

If you find out what is wrong and clear it up, you will not have the pain. But you have to survive until that happens. So you may need an operation, you may need some medicine, you may need some therapy, you may need a chiropractor, you may need a dentist. That is not a violation of the Word.

God never told you not to go to a doctor or use a dentist. All God says is, *do not look at the problem*! I did not let the dry socket, or my foot, tell me when and when not to preach. I let God tell me when and when not to preach. Do you understand the difference? So in the meantime, if I need something, I take a pill. But sometimes, like I said, the attacks come on you when you are not in a position to get the pill. Do you understand what I am saying? I call those things which do not exist as though they did.

If I believe that I am well, I have to act well, think well and talk well. In the meantime, I deny the right of the things which are seen to dictate or tell me what to do. But I may need to do something about those symptoms. Take the pill, take some medication, go to the dentist or whatever you have to do.

Faith Works With Medicine

Faith is not in opposition to medication. What you need to understand is that medication is not a cure-all. God has already built healing into your body. And given all the proper parameters, your body will heal itself.

But sometimes the damage and devastation to your flesh can be so overwhelming at the time, your body cannot recover fast enough before it is destroyed, so you may need some medication or perhaps an operation to keep you alive until your faith, working with the natural healing already built into your body, can bring itself back to where it ought to be.

Aspirins do not heal headaches. All they do is mask the pain. It is not taking away the cause of the pain, because as I said, pain is symptomatic. Pain is the effect and whatever is wrong with you is the cause. If you eliminate the cause you will have no effect.

If I have a sore throat, I do not deny that I have a sore throat, I just do not go around talking about the sore throat. I talk about what God says about the sore throat. God says I am well, so I confess that I believe that I am well. Now in the meantime, if I can take something that will give me some relief, I do it until my faith drives whatever is wrong with me, out of my body.

Healing Is a Progression

Everything in terms of healing does not happen instantaneously. Jesus said it Himself in Mark 16:17,18:

And these signs will follow those who believe: In My name...they will lay hands on the sick, and they will recover.

The very word *recover* means *progression*. It did not say that they will lay hands on the sick and they will instantly be healed or changed. No, He said they will recover. *Recover* means to go from the point of being sick to the point of being well.

How long will that take? I do not know, because I do not know where your level of faith is. I do not know the nature of your condition. Some conditions take more faith to remove them, because it is your faith that does it.

It is easier for your faith to dry up a runny nose than it is to remove a tumor. There is a difference. It will do it, but it may take longer than you can afford to wait at the time.

Most of the time when you find out about these things you never find out one second after the tumor begins to develop. If you did, you could knock it out every time, and no one would ever die of cancer. Ninety-nine times out of a hundred, when you find out there is something wrong, it is too late, in the natural. It has such a head start on you, you cannot catch up!

It is like a sporting event. For example, let us assume you were running in the Olympic games as a sprinter in the one-hundred meter dash, and let us say you are the world champion and had run faster than anyone before. If I ran against you, and certainly I am not an Olympic one-hundred meter champion, and I started at the seventy-five meter mark and you started at zero, there is no way you can catch me before I reach the finish line. I do not care how fast you can run. There would not be enough time for you to make up the difference before I crossed the finish line.

Here is my point. Sometimes this is what happens with disease and sickness. They have such a head start on you, I do not care how fast you run, you cannot catch up. There is not enough time to the end of the race for you to catch up, not with that kind of a head start. And that is what cancer and many of these diseases do. Once they get a hold of you, you had better find a doctor and get some medication. Do not sit around trying to use your faith.

Some of you have already been told that you have a tumor, but you are afraid of the doctor, afraid of the operation, so you have not gone to the doctor and the tumor keeps growing and growing and you are calling it faith. It is more like foolishness, so you had better get some help. Remember, fear is not faith!

17

Teach Faith to Your Children

2 Corinthians 4:18:
While we do not look at the things which are seen, but at the things which are not seen. For the things which are seen are temporary, but the things which are not seen are eternal.

Earlier, I gave you a paraphrase of this verse that I think helps to make it clearer than what it might appear in the Bible. I pointed out to you that the word *seen* is not talking about visual perception. And that is what we have a tendency to think of—what we see visually, or from the standpoint of our senses.

What he is talking about is the difference between sensory perception and spiritual perception. Even though I discussed it before, I want to go over this one more time and add some things to it that I believe will be helpful to you. This is the way I paraphrased it:

"While we *do not* look at the things which are perceived by the senses, but at the things which are not perceived by the senses, for or because, the things which are perceived by the senses are temporal, temporary or subject to change. But the things which are not perceived by the senses are eternal and everlasting."

If you are going to walk by faith, you cannot allow what you see in the sense realm to dictate the terms of your existence. Remember again, we do not deny the things in the sense realm. They are there, they are real, but they have nothing to do with our faith, unless we allow them to.

The way that we allow them to, is by letting them tell us how to act, what to say, and what to do. We should be letting God by His Word tell us that. When we let God, by His Word tell us, then that is faith.

Now I want to deal with one other point in reference to Second Corinthians 4:18 before we leave it because it is such a misunderstood point. We are to live our lives by faith.

The problem for many people is, when they found out about living by faith, their lives were already in motion. They were already down the road of life, and they had already put into operation some things that they did not realize they were putting into operation, by what they were believing and by what they were saying with their mouths, over a lifetime.

Let me give you an illustration. I would wager that most people reading this who are adults, when they found out about the principles of tithing, were already in financial deprivation. Most of us were like that. We had bills up to our eyeballs. We had credit that was stringing us out. We were already financially out of it. We wanted to tithe, but we could not tithe *and* pay the bills. So something had to give.

Naturally, since we cannot see God and He does not come down here and repossess anything, we figured we could miss paying God. But we had better pay the creditors, because they will come and get the car. They will foreclose on our house, so we had better pay them. Now because we are already in a credit buying mode, it is very difficult for some people to get into a position where they can begin to tithe.

If a person was trained from childhood to tithe, there would be no problem. I have a teenage son and he already knows about tithing. If he does not do what he knows when he grows up, he will get his behind kicked by life. But he had the advantage to learn about this as a child. I did not.

When I found out about it, I was already in debtor's prison, so to speak. I was out on bail. I had to play catch up. Had all of us become Christians as children and if we had been taught as children, then we would not have to play catch up down the road.

We did not find out about divine healing, or about walking by faith, until we were already adults. And we had been sewing seeds that had opened the door for the enemy to have a right to put things on us all of our lives without realizing it. So now we find out about faith; now we find out about with Jesus' stripes we were healed.

But now what do I do? I get physically attacked with something, and so I attempt to use my faith on it, but do not get any instant results.

Remember the illustration about the track meet? The thing has such a big head start on me, if there is not some divine intervention, then I may die, if I have some kind of terminal condition. It did not start the minute it was diagnosed as terminal. The diagnosis is the result of things that have already been in operation over time.

Look at the Word of God

The question in reference to faith is, "How do I operate now?" He tells me, **do not look at the things which are seen.** But I have pain. The X-ray says I have this growth as big as a grapefruit. What am I supposed to do? God said not to look at it. That is right. You do not look at it.

You look at the Word of God. But what you have to realize is that God's Word is for God's people. But it is for God's people as babies—as little children. That is the reason why the writer in Proverbs said, *train up.* He did not say, "Train up an adult." He said, **Train up a *child* in the way he should go...** (Prov. 22:6).

But how in the world can Christian parents train their children in the things of the Lord, when most Christians do not know themselves and are not walking in it as adults? They go to churches where they have never been taught or instructed. They were told, "Hold on to God's unchanging hand." So they do not know, and therefore cannot train their children.

Things begin to work in our lives and then all of a sudden, we find ourselves with something. Now what do we do? We have to get out of the situation, but how? When He tells us not to look at the things which are seen, He is telling us that we have to look at God's Word.

I may claim something by faith, because the Word says so. But while I am waiting for the manifestation, this thing is the size of a grapefruit and is pushing against some area in my body, causing me great pain. My body is not functioning right. What am I supposed to do about that?

Don't Be Afraid to See a Doctor

Let me answer that by way of illustration. Someone came up in the healing line for me to minister to them for healing. They told me what was wrong with them. Come to find out, the person wanted me to pray for them, wanted healing in other words, not because they believed that God would heal them through that method, but they were afraid of the doctor.

They were afraid of an operation, radiation treatments and chemotherapy. They had heard horror stories about it, so they did not want to go through that. They thought that they would come up for healing, because they did not want to be cut on.

If that growth is as big as a grapefruit, it is obvious it has a head start on you. We have had people in our congregation, especially women, who had a little knot about the size of a green pea in their breast, but were afraid of an operation, afraid of treatments. They were just going to believe God.

How are you going to believe for it to leave when your faith is not strong enough to keep it from coming? Besides that, even if your faith had been strong enough to keep it from coming, you might have been doing something dumb without knowing you were doing it that made a contribution to Satan having a legal right to put that on you.

I do not care if you have faith as tall as Mount Everest, and if you pray on the hour every hour, you are still going to die or the doctor is going to have to help to save your life. Your faith cannot work if you are doing something that is violating a law, either spiritual or physical.

In the meantime, until you find out, you had better get some help. Some of these women have died when they could have been saved. And I am not talking about women on a deathbed. I am talking about young, vibrant, good-looking women, with a little knot in their breast, but afraid to go to a doctor. That growth kept getting bigger and bigger.

They were talking about what they were believing. "I believe I am healed." The growth was getting bigger and bigger. They were operating in fear, not faith, because they kept coming back for prayer.

It is obvious they were not truly believing, because if you really believed you were healed, you would not come up for prayer again. All these are tell-tale signs that ought to let you know to get to your doctor, until the power of God is able to drive that thing out of your body.

He said, **While we look not at the things which are seen....** *He did not say, "Do not get some treatments," He did not say, "Do not have an operation." He did not say, "Do not take some medicine." He just said, "Do not look at it."*

Let God's Word Dictate Your Actions

Do not look at it in the sense of letting it dictate what you do. You let God's Word do that. But in the meantime you may need some help with the symptoms. Remember, pain is symptomatic. It is not causative.

Pain is a symptom telling you that something is wrong with you. You need to check it out. You need to find out what is wrong with you, so that you can do something about it. Otherwise you may end up dying.

God does not want you to die. Why do you think He gave us doctors? You do not think the devil invented doctors, do you? You do not think the devil invented medicine, do you? No, God did.

God did this to help His children who do not have their faith developed to the point of being able to do something about their condition, and who may not even know that they are making a contribution to their own illness.

A case in point is my wife. I have lived with the lady for forty years. There is not a kinder, sweeter, more compassionate woman than my wife. If there is any human who could be called good, it is my wife. Good all the time. Never anything bad. I guess I could call her *perfect* like God called Job perfect. We know he was not perfect (flawless), but God did say Job was perfect and upright.

My wife is that woman. And yet this cancer came on her body. She is a faith woman. Her husband is a faith teacher—Dr. Frederick K.C. Price. The FaithDome preacher. The television preacher. Yet my wife was stricken. That was the thing that stymied me. That was the thing that had me confused.

I could not understand it, because I was looking at the moral part—the spiritual part. And there was absolutely no way, no reason why she could be attacked from that standpoint.

But we had not thought about the physical part. We had not thought about the things *she was not doing*, all of her life, that she should have been doing. Like flushing her system out with water. She never drank water. If she drank one quart of water in forty years, it would have been a miracle.

She did not like water, so she would not drink it. Who in the world would have ever thought that drinking water would have that much to do with a cancer or anything like that?

I do not intend to be offensive by being graphic, but I only want to help people. She never had proper bowel elimination. She was eating ill combined foods all of her life, just like most people. And so without realizing it, she opened the door to the enemy. This was not an issue, nothing spiritual, but purely physical, and we did not even know it.

No one had really taught us about nutrition. Generally speaking, you do not learn it in school. In fact most of the medical profession is not even taught nutrition in medical school. And so we did not know. And almost anything we can get in our mouths, we put in, not realizing that we are poisoning our own systems, many times, by the methods and the way that we eat.

All that behavior can have a cumulative effect on our bodies over years. Flesh breaks at that point and then you have an intrusion. Satan will feed on it, and use it as a doorway to destroy you.

Even if you do not know that you are doing what you are doing to your body—even if God worked a miracle in you, and you got healed instantaneously—you will get the same thing or something worse next time. Why do I say that? Because you have not changed the thing that opened the door for the problem to come in the first place. If you do not change, the problem is coming back again.

The only way it does not come back is to cut the leg off. Now you cannot get gangrene, not in that leg, because you no longer have the leg. If you take out the organ, naturally, it cannot be diseased anymore.

Sin Kills

If you do not think this principle works, why did Jesus say to the man who was at the pool of Bethesda, after He found him in the temple, "You are whole now. Do not sin anymore lest something worse comes on you" (John 5:14, author's paraphrase). So our actions are important, and it is not always moral sin that destroys us or kills us.

Understand this, it is a sin to abuse your body. Your body was bought with the blood of Jesus. It belongs to God. It is not your property. And yet you are messing it up and befouling it all the time. That is a sin. It is a sin to continually eat wrong. It is a sin to be overweight.

It is a sin to stuff yourself until your flesh can hardly carry the weight. It is a sin in the realm of the physical, and you are going to pay a price. Judgment day is coming.

In fact, some people are already paying the price. They can hardly move around without pain. Much of it is a result of them abusing their body. Let me show you a Scripture that some of you do not know.

1 Corinthians 6:19,20:

> **Or do you not know that your body is the temple of the Holy Spirit who is in you, whom you have from God, and you are not your own? For you were bought at a price; therefore glorify God in your body and in your spirit, which are God's.**

Whatever I pay my money for, I purchase. It then becomes mine. Jesus has bought and paid for you. You belong to Him. You are His property. How are you treating His property?

Your body and your spirit belong to God. When you abuse that body, that is sin. Yes, *that is sin!* And you are going to pay a price, because *the wages of sin is death.* Sometimes it is instant death like a heart attack, because you have been messing over your body. And sometimes it is long term, like a cancer that develops over the years.

But the wages of sin is death. And so, you come up, and you want to get prayed for. You are afraid of the doctor, the knife, the treatments. That is not faith. There is no hope for you, unless you get to the doctor and let him help you. And understand this, *faith is not against the doctors, and doctors are not against faith as such.* It is not God's best.

Driving a car from Los Angeles to New York is not the best way to go. You could fly first class. But I guarantee you can get there in a car. It is better to get there in a car than not to get there at all.

So even though the surgeon's knife may not be God's best, thank God it is available to help you until you can get to the point where you can truly exercise your faith on a level that would bring divine healing to your body.

No, you do not look at the things which are seen, you look at the things that are not seen. By the Word of God, I believe that I am healed. But if I need some help, if I need something for the pain which is symptomatic, which is only a result of the cause, I take it, while my faith is applied to the cause. And, of course, if it is imminent, you may need to have the cause removed, or you are going to die.

God is not going to get any glory out of you dying. So you may need some help. You may need medicine; you may need an operation; you may need some treatments.

Thank God those things were available for my wife, or she would have died, because she was killing herself and did not know it. That is like saying, "I didn't know the gun was loaded." The guy is lying in the floor dead. It did not matter whether he knew the gun was loaded, he is still dead.

Ignorance Is No Excuse

Ignorance is no excuse. You are still dead. And so she was killing herself and did not know it. Sweetest person in the world, and yet doing it to herself—sinning against her flesh. There is a price to pay. The wages of sin is death.

Satan, of course, came right in and utilized the opportunity to kill her. But thank God she had the Word. She had so much Word in her that she was able to stand against the biggest thing that kills most people which is the fear.

Satan uses the fear to kill most people. They die from either a combination of the fear of the tumor, the knife, the radiation, the chemotherapy, or the amputation. Either way, Satan and the fear still kill them.

But because my wife had the Word in her (because she did not know what was wrong with her, or why it was wrong with her), no fear came to her. The devil could not use the situation and capitalize on it.

During that time, God moved on the heart of a TV viewer to send us a book, *Fit for Life*, by Harvey and Marilyn Diamond. That was the open door.

As soon as we read the book we had our answer. We were eating ourselves to death and did not know it. You are making all the right confessions and still getting sick. You wonder why that is? Because there may be something you are doing or not doing in the physical you do not realize.

We do not need to just know spiritual things, we need to know some things ourselves. We need a combination of all of these things. God has made a physical body, and we have to take care of it. If you do not, your body will break down.

If you keep driving your car and never put any oil in it, after a while that car is going to heat up and freeze up on you. If you need some help, *get it*! To get some help is not in opposition to your faith, *unless* you put your faith in that help, and not in God. I am looking to God to keep me well, but I may have to use this, that or the other to deal with the symptoms.

I am looking to God to deal with the source through my faith, and then I am seeking the Lord to show me what I need to do, and show me where I am missing it, if I am missing it in the natural realm. I am not talking about spiritually. But there are so many things physically that we do not know about.

The Bible says we are fearfully and wonderfully made. Our bodies are made so well, we can still end up living sixty and seventy years with total abuse to the body. That is how good a piece of equipment God has made. You can kick it in the behind, you can abuse it— never change the oil as it were—and it will still last sixty, seventy, eighty years. Can you imagine what would happen if we treated our bodies right!

But how can you if you do not know how. "We've always eaten this. Our family was raised on this." Raised on the wrong things. It has a cumulative effect. Over the years it will take its toll. That is what happened to my wife. She was putting it in, and not letting it out. The waste has to go somewhere.

After food has been digested, or even if it has not been digested properly, there will be some toxic waste. If those toxic wastes are not flushed down the toilet, they are going to find some other outlet in your body. She went all those years without proper elimination, only now and then having a bowel movement. Where did that waste go? It will fester somewhere inside. Wherever there is a weak opening, that is where it is going to start developing.

You may be doing something and not realize it. You have all your prayers right. You are believing right, confessing right. And here comes this thing out of the blue, as it were. I mean there could have been a weakness in your flesh when you were born. You know what I mean? Veins or something like that could just be weak, because of heredity and other things like that. But I am talking about things that we have control over, that *we* could do.

Thank God we found out what was wrong, and we closed that door on the devil. He could not use that against her anymore. And thank God for the doctors. Thank God for the operations. Thank God for the chemotherapy. No! No! There is nothing pleasant about it. Nothing good about it, in the sense that, who wants to go through it? Nobody!

Most really reputable doctors even hate to give it to you, but that is all they have at this point. They know what it is going to do to you. It can destroy good cells in your body. But the main thing is that it destroys the tumor. And, of course, with God working with you and your faith working, He can accelerate the healing process and that is what He did with my wife.

Her oncologist said it was a miracle. He had not seen anyone respond like she did. The thing just about disappeared the first week of treatments. Now, it is going to cost you something. You have to get past all the junk that Satan will bring against your mind.

"Oh, if I have to take chemotherapy I am going to lose all my hair. I do not want to lose my hair." Well, if you do not get some help, you are going to lose your *life*. What good does a dead body full of hair do anyone? I would rather be alive and bald, than dead with a head full of hair. Give me life. Forget the hair. Are you going to die over some hair? Get a wig! My wife lost all her hair, but you should see her now. She does not wear a wig. Her hair grew back.

You cannot sit around and wait for a miracle; God wants us to walk by faith.

18

God Is Known by Faith

Ephesians 1:3:

> **Blessed be the God and Father of our Lord Jesus Christ, who has blessed us with every spiritual blessing in the heavenly places in Christ.**

If God *has* blessed us, then He cannot bless us tomorrow. *Has* means He has already done it. Therefore, we are already blessed. So when we say, "The Lord bless you," it is like saying, "He has not blessed you."

Faith says He has already done it because He said, **...who has blessed us with every spiritual blessing in the heavenly places in Christ.** I like that—*every*. How much is left out of the word *every*? It does not leave anything out. It says *every*.

If He had said, "Who has blessed us with *some* blessing," we would know that there are some other things that are not included in "has blessed." Is that right? But thank God, He says *every*.

Here is the key in this verse: **...who has blessed us with every spiritual blessing in the heavenly places in Christ.** Great, Lord! Wonderful! Thank You, Father, for having blessed us with every spiritual blessing in heavenly places.

But Father, I am not in heavenly places. I am in this three-dimensional physical world. Father, I am not in the spirit world, so I do not need a spiritual blessing. My roof is leaking. All four of my tires are bald. Even the bald is bald.

199

It is wonderful that You have blessed me in heavenly places with every spiritual blessing, but I need some tires. I need a new roof on my house. It is almost time for the children to go back to school, and they have outgrown all their clothes. I need some clothes for the kids, and I do not have sufficient money.

It is wonderful that You have blessed me with every spiritual blessing in heavenly places, but how does that affect tomorrow morning, when I have to go to the store to buy for the kids and I not have the money? Do you see where I am coming from? This is where we live, not in heavenly places! What about *now*? Good question. This is why this subject is so important.

We want to find out why God requires us to believe that we receive something that we cannot see, and then have to wait for it to physically manifest in this three-dimensional world.

Why not just deliver it to my front door and let me see it? I would not have to believe it, I would know it. Why do we have to go through this? Because that is the way God has designed the system. And once you understand how the system works, you can very easily plug into it.

There Are Two Realms

I told you that there are two worlds, or two realms: the spirit world and the physical, three-dimensional world. The spirit world is more real than the three-dimensional physical world. The physical or three-dimensional world is the result, or the effect of the cause, which is Almighty God in the spirit world.

In the fourth chapter of John, Jesus is talking to a woman at Jacob's well, outside the small town of Sychar. In the course of the conversation, they get into a dialogue about spiritual values. Jesus makes this very revealing statement in verse 24:

God is Spirit, and those who worship Him must worship in spirit and truth.

Jesus says that God is Spirit. Then in the gospel of John, chapter 1, verse 1, it says, **In the beginning was the Word....**

The Greek word for *Word* as used in this verse is *logos*. It means the second person of the Godhead, or Jesus Christ in eternity past. It is talking about Christ. Biblical scholars at least agree that the *Logos* is the Son of God.

It says, **In the beginning was the Word** (or, was the Son of God), **and the Word was with God....** If anyone ought to know Who God is and What God is, it ought to be Whoever was with Him in the beginning.

God Is a Spirit

Since Jesus was with Him in the beginning, and Jesus says that God is Spirit, then God must be Spirit.

In the *King James Version* (which I think is a better rendering of this verse), Jesus said that God **is a Spirit.** He did not say that God *is* Spirit. He said **God is a Spirit.** There is a difference. It is not a play on words, but a very important distinction.

The reason that He says it that way is because angels are spirits. Demons are spirits. And man is a spirit. You are a spirit. Jesus said, **God is a Spirit.**

Man Made in "Our Image and Likeness"

Let us now go to the book of beginnings.

Genesis 1:26:

Then God said, "Let Us make man in Our image, according to Our likeness....

Us is plural, indicative of or indicating at least one other person with God in order to be an *Us*. The *Us* was the corporate officers of *God and company*. God the Father (Chief Executive Officer), Jesus, the Son of God, (Executive

Vice-President), and the Holy Spirit, (Field Representative). That is the *Us*.

God said, **Let Us....** [Father, Son, and Holy Spirit....] **Let Us make man in Our....** God did not say, "Let Us make man in *My* image," He said, **Let Us make man in *Our* image....**

Each one in the Godhead must be of the same species. In other words, one is not a flea, another a dog, and one a banana. They must all be the same. Whatever they are, they must be the same. Because He said, Let Us make man in *Our* image, not in *My image*. Jesus said **...God is a Spirit**.

If God is a Spirit, then Jesus is a Spirit, and the Holy Spirit is a Spirit. That means we must be spirits in order to be made in the image and likeness of God. What is God like? God is a Spirit. I am a spirit, and so are you. You are an ever-living, never-dying, eternally existing spirit. As long as God *is*, we are.

Since God is a Spirit, then everything started out in the spirit world. Everything has a spiritual basis to it. This three-dimensional physical world is only a replica of what was in the mind of God in the spirit world. Genesis 1:1 says, **In the beginning God created the heavens and the earth.**

If God created the heavens and the earth, He would have to already be in existence to create the world. You have what is called cause and effect. God is the cause and the universe is the effect.

Since God is a Spirit, and God created the world, or the universe, then the spirit must be more real than the universe that was created by the Spirit, because it does not take the creation to keep the Creator in existence, but it does take the Creator to keep the creation in existence. Now, follow along, because this is very important.

If everything that is in the physical realm came from the spirit realm, then everything in the physical realm had to be in the mind of God before God could create it. When the Bible says, **Then God said, Let there be**, it had to already be in God's mind what the earth was going to look like, because there were a number of options.

The earth does not have to be spherical. It could be a square or cube. It could be diamond-shaped or even a rectangle. But He created a sphere. So when God said, **Let there be**, that had to already be in the mind of God, so that when He spoke it into existence, He would know, "That is what I spoke."

The Physical World Is a Reflection of the Spiritual

Everything in the physical world was first of all in the spirit world in the mind of God, and then God spoke it into existence. When God said, "Let the animals be," He must have had in His mind what a giraffe would look like when He created it, or He would not have known that it was a giraffe and not a dog. Everything that we see in the natural world *started* in the spirit world. *Everything has its origin in the spirit world.*

Everything has its origin in the spirit world and that is why we have to use faith. Because everything that we need, and everything that we desire that would be consistent with a godly life was in the mind of God before it was created. Everything!

Fords were in the mind of God. Boeing 747 Jetliners were in the mind of God. Concord Jetliners were in the mind of God. Golf clubs were in the mind of God. Television was in the mind of God. AM/FM radios were in the mind of God. Clothes were in the mind of God. Shoes were in the mind of God. Diamond rings were in the mind of God. Earrings were in the mind of God. Glasses were in the mind of God.

Man has no ability to *create* anything! All man can do is mimic what was placed inside of him. Man has not created anything. We have no creative ability. Everything that we see had to be in God and then God put it in us, so that we could bring it out in this physical, three-dimensional world for our benefit.

Everything Begins in the Mind of God

Notice the progressive steps—spirit world and then the physical world. It has to be in the mind of God. In fact, if you stop and think about it, everything around your room, and on yourself, was first of all in the mind of someone before it was manifested. Someone has to have the thought in their mind for a suit, dress, carpet, etc.

When a building is constructed, it did not just pop up out of nowhere. The thought was in someone's mind as to what the building would finally look like. Then an architect put it on paper, so that the construction people could get a visual of what they were going to build. They had to have construction drawings, so they would know what to put here and what to put there, so that the final product would look like the blueprint.

Everything, in reality, is in the mind of someone. Then that is in the mind of God, because God put us in this world.

Go back to Ephesians 1:3:

Who has blessed us with every spiritual blessing in the heavenly places in Christ.

Your roof is a spiritual thing. Your four bald tires are spiritual things. Your clothes for the kids going back to school are spiritual things. That money that you need to pay your taxes is a spiritual thing. It starts out in the spirit world, and is manifested in this three-dimensional, physical world.

I am talking about Christians relating to God. I am not talking about the natural realm, or people in the natural, because money is already here. Cars and many other things are already here but you do not have them.

There are many things that you desire, but do not have the money to buy them now, and you may never have the money, in the natural, to buy them. You may want to buy something, but do not have the money. That is all that stands between you and it, unless someone gives it to you.

There are some wonderful things that man has manufactured, based upon the vision that God placed in man when God created man. But man, outside of God, does not realize it. He does not know it. He thinks he is coming up with these ideas on his own.

When man listens to malevolent spirits, Satan or demons, then the vision that God has placed in man's heart to bring forth becomes distorted. That is why we have all the bad things in the world, which are a distortion of the good.

There is no bad in God. But because He created us with a free will, then gave us dominion over His creation, what we have here is our fault. If there is going to be any changes, we will have to make them, because He gave us the authority to do so.

Look at Genesis 1:26 again:

> **Then God said, "Let Us make man in Our image, according to Our likeness; let them have dominion over the fish of the sea, over the birds of the air, and over the cattle, over all the earth and over every creeping thing that creeps on the earth."**

What is dominion? What does the word *dominion* mean? It means control. It means you are the boss, you are in charge. Right? **Let them have....** In other words, we rule. We are not to be ruled, we are to rule (but not each other).

205

Dominion.... Where, Father? Over the fish of the sea, over the birds of the air, and over the cattle, over all the earth (gold, silver, oil, minerals, etc.) **and over every creeping thing that creeps on the earth.**

God put us in charge. If we do not listen to God and find out how all this is supposed to work, then it becomes distorted. And that is why you have the bad things. If there is any good to be done, we have to do it. God is not going to do it, because He has given us the authority to do it. There is a malevolent spirit, Satan, who wants to keep things in turmoil.

You can operate by the Spirit of God, through the Word of God by faith, and you can make things good for your own personal life. No individual can make it good for the whole world, but you can make it good for your own personal life. You can make your own Garden of Eden. God wants you to have it.

Faith Makes the Transfer

Everything that we need or desire is out there in that spirit world. By our faith, we make the transfer for our benefit, into this three-dimensional, physical world. Either you get the things, or you get the money to buy the things—one of the two.

If you have been working on a job any length of time, you should already recognize that you are not going to get ahead. Most people work for someone else. They do not have their own business, so they are not the boss. They are not the president of the company.

You ought to be able to recognize by now that the economic systems of the world are not designed for you to get ahead. They are presided over by Satan. He is in control of them, because Adam gave him control of the world when Adam sinned.

Jesus came and purchased the world system back for the family of God, but it has not yet been instituted worldwide. The potential is there for you as an individual to have your piece of the pie. But you have to get it by exercising your faith.

Let me say it again. The world economic system is not designed for you to get ahead. It is designed to keep you chained to the wheels of industry, so that those who are in control can grow richer, and you can grow older.

You cannot get ahead in the system—not legally. It is not designed for you to legally get ahead, because if you get ahead legally, you become independent. And if you become independent, you cannot be controlled anymore. So if they can keep you under control, they can manipulate you the way they want, so that they can enjoy the benefits of your work and labor.

Most of the people who work daily jobs are not doctors, lawyers, or professional people. Those kinds of people make it pretty well, but that is just a very small percentage of the working force. The rest of the people are working for someone else.

It is amazing how things change over the years relative to the economic systems of the world. I remember when the goal of the working class was to ascend the hourly wage scale to *one dollar* an hour. That is right. When you made a dollar an hour you had arrived.

The goal of the working professional was to become what was called a ten-thousand-dollar-a-year man. That was the man in the gray flannel suit. That was it! You may think I am kidding you, but I am not.

One dollar an hour! If you made a dollar an hour, you were living, as they say, *high on the hog*. In fact you *owned* the hog! You had a vested interest in the hog. Is that incredible or not?

My wife and I have been married for over forty years. Forty years ago we could buy groceries for a whole week for ten dollars. What could you do now if that was all you had to pay for groceries? You would have all kinds of money left.

Forty years ago I could buy gas for sixteen cents a gallon. Ten cents for a loaf of bread. Is that awesome or not? Think where you would be today at those prices. We would all be rich. But *they* will not let you do that.

Notice how they have correspondingly raised the prices on *everything*. Sure, they let you make five dollars an hour. You think you are making something. Right? But you pay three dollars for a loaf of bread.

You think you are doing something now, making thirty-thousand dollars a year. Right? But you are paying almost two dollars a gallon for gas, and it will keep going higher. After a while, you will be making five thousand dollars a week, but it will cost you twenty five dollars for a gallon of gas.

If you ever become financially independent of the circumstances, on Monday morning you just might decide to go yachting instead of going to the office and punching that computer terminal. If you do that, the finance moguls are not going to get any richer. They do not want you to get ahead. They have to keep you tied to that machine.

But they want to encourage you. They will hand you a carrot now and then. They will give you just enough to make you think you are making some headway. They will give you that twenty-five dollar an hour raise. They will let you make $40,000 a year, and you will think you are doing something. You are not doing anything, because the price of everything goes up correspondingly.

There are some of you who are reading this book and you are making more money now than you ever made in your whole life, and you are still not making enough. With all the money you are making, I will guarantee you that not a person in a hundred is saving half of their weekly paycheck.

You are probably like most working people, living up to every nickel and dime you make. But I have good news for you. There is a place in God where you can rise above the circumstances of life. But you will have to learn to walk by faith and not by sight. I have done it. That is why I am so gung-ho on it.

I have done it, and that is why I take the time to share it with you. It is workable. It is feasible and you can do it. The system will not let you, but *faith* will, because all the necessary ingredients are here.

They are manufacturing *things* every day. They are making new models every day. It is not like it is not there, but you do not have the money to get it. You can get it in Christ. Now, those things are not the end. Jesus is the end. The Christ life is the end. But He said, **I have come that they may have life, and that they may have it more abundantly** (John 10:10). The abundance goes with the life. He does not want you to just have life, to live here, die and go to heaven.

Heaven Is Not the Goal

Heaven is not the goal. People say, "Well, so-and-so died and went home to be with the Lord." *They did not go home.* They were already home. *This is home!* Heaven is not home. Heaven is a staging area. It is a temporary place.

You were not created for heaven, you are created for this earth. That is why you have an earth suit called a body. You do not need a physical body in heaven, because that is the spirit world. All you would need is your pure spirit body, but in this three-dimensional world, you need an earth suit called a body.

You were created for this earth, and the earth was created for you. Not for God, for you. So you will eventually be here forever—if you are child of God—and you will reign with Christ.

If you are not a child of God, you will be in the lake, and I do not mean Lake Michigan or Lake Superior. I am talking about *the* lake, the one with fire and brimstone in it. So you say, "I don't believe in that." Fine. When you get there, send me a postcard because you are going there if you do not know Jesus.

God wants you to have this life and have it in style. Consider this, how do you think God lives? Do you think God is getting a welfare check every week? Do you think God lives on skid row? No! He could not want any less for His children than He wants for Himself.

Look at you, with your little pea-sized, penny-pinching brain! You want more for your children than you have for yourself. I want my son to be a millionaire. I want him to be a multi-millionaire. I want my children, all of them, to succeed. And I am working on it with all I can, to impact on their lives so that their lives will exceed mine.

Just like me, you want more for your children, too. Where do you think that idea came from? It came from the original Father—the Father God. You cannot love your kids any more than God loves His children.

Everything Is Activated by Faith

Because of the way He has designed this system to work, everything is activated by faith. It is a simple principle to understand, comparatively speaking.

Everything in this physical, three-dimensional world, is activated by dollars. Coin of the realm. Money. That is all. You can have anything that is manufactured or that you can commission to be manufactured—all you need is enough money.

They will make robots for you—they have the technology to do it. Whatever you can think of, man can make. All you have to do is have the money. That is all that stands between you and it. Money!

In this economic world that we live in, all that it takes to make your dreams come true and to have all of your desires met (I am talking about the natural now) is enough money. Any place in this world, or on this planet that you have ever thought you might want to see, there is someone who will take you there.

They will fly you there on the world's fastest jetliner (the Concord) if you want them to. They will take you in a boat. They will fly you by helicopter. Have you ever been to Hawaii? Would you like to go? If you would like to go and have never been to Hawaii, or wherever, I will prophesy and tell you why you have never been there.

"Thus says the Lord, you have not been to Hawaii because you could not afford to go to Hawaii!" All that has stood between most of you going was the money. Am I right or not? I am not trying to be funny. I am just using that as an analogy. If you can understand that, then flip that over to the spirit realm, and the thing that works in the spirit realm instead of dollars is *faith*.

If you have enough dollars in this life, you can have anything your heart desires. Anything that they make, and whatever they have not made yet, they will manufacture it for you. You can commission it to be made.

Faith Is the Currency of the Kingdom

In the Kingdom of God, faith is like dollars in the economic or three-dimensional world. Faith makes everything work. The more faith you have going in the spirit world, the more dollars you have going in the physical world. Can you understand that?

Let me show you very graphically, that there are things existing in the spirit world, even though we cannot see them physically. I want to give you a biblical illustration of it.

Elisha Showed His Servant the Spirit World

I will give you a paraphrase of Second Kings 6:8-17, because it is a lengthy story.

At this particular time in the history of the nation of Israel, Israel was at war with Syria. The Syrian troops would go out to do battle, or engage the armies of Israel in battle.

There was a prophet in the land at that time, and God would speak to that prophet and give him the revelation of the battle plans of the Syrian army. The armies of Israel would go out and set up ambushes against the armies of Syria, and every time the armies of Syria would attempt to engage the armies of Israel in battle, their plans would be known ahead of time, and they would be thwarted in their attempts to overtake Israel.

Finally, the king of Syria said, "You know, we must have a traitor in our midst. Somebody is giving away our military secrets." One of the officers said, "No king, that's not the problem at all. There's a prophet over in Israel and he knows everything—even what's going on in your bed chamber." (He really did not. He only knew what God revealed to him.)

The king said, "Where is he?" And the officer said, "He's in the city of Dothan, in Samaria." And the king said, "Get the troops together. We are going to lay siege against that city while it's still dark. Then, in the morning, we will blast that place off the map, and do away with this break in our communications."

That night they came and laid siege against the city of Dothan. (In those days, most of the cities were built with walls around them for fortification.) So they laid siege against the city that night, waiting for the dawn so that they could go into the city and destroy it.

The prophet, Elisha, had a servant named Gehazi. One of his jobs was to draw water daily from the well because they did not have in-house running water. So the servant went out that morning to do what he always did. And because it was such a beautiful day, he said, "Man, this is just fabulous. What a day this is. I think I am going to go up onto the wall, and look over into the valley."

It was harvest time, the crops were about to come in, and everything was looking good. He said, "I think I will go up on the wall and check things out." When he got up on the wall, his eyeballs almost fell out of their sockets. As far as his eyes could see, the valleys, the mountainsides, the rivers, the bridge, every place was covered with the armies of Syria. In fact, it looked like a plague of locusts. They were everywhere.

The servant dropped his water buckets and ran back to the house hollering and screaming, "My master, my master, my master, what shall we do, what shall we do? The armies of Syria, the armies of Syria. We're surrounded. We're gonna die. There's no way out. What are we gonna do?" And the prophet grabbed him by the shoulders and said, "Man, get yourself together. What's wrong with you?! Sit down here and have a cup of hot chocolate and a couple of crumb donuts."

After the servant had his third cup of hot chocolate with a little whipped cream on top, a little cinnamon sprinkled on that, and his third crumb donut, the prophet said, "All right now. Take it from the top. Run it through again."

"My master, I went out to draw water as I usually do. It was such a beautiful day, when I got outside I decided I was going to go up on the wall of the city. When I got up to the wall and looked into the valley, all I could see were the armies of Syria. I saw their flag-bearers and their flag standards. My master, there is no way out. We are going to die here in Dothan. We can't get out. We're completely surrounded."

The prophet said, "Take me out and show me what you are talking about." So they finally got up on the wall, and the servant said, "See, look my master." And the prophet said, "Oh." The servant looked at him and said, "Oh? Is that *all* you can say? We are about to die, we are surrounded, and all you can say is *oh*? **So he answered, "Do not fear, for those who are with us are more than those who are with them"** (v. 16).

Now about this time the servant stepped back from the prophet assuredly thinking that a lightning bolt was going to strike and blow him away. And the servant began to count. Ten-thousand, twenty-thousand, thirty-thousand, forty, fifty, sixty, seventy, eighty, ninety, one-hundred, one-hundred and ten-thousand picked Syrian troops. He turned to the prophet and said, "One, two." A hundred and ten-thousand, "One, two."

He stepped back a little further, and said, "He must be crazy, maybe he had a sunstroke. Can't he see, a hundred and ten-thousand of them and two of us, and he's talking about there's more with us than are with them." Keep in mind, dear reader, *while we look not at the things which are perceived by the senses, but at the things which are not perceived by the senses. For we walk by the Word and not by the senses.*

The Eyes of the Spirit Must Be Opened

And Elisha prayed, and said, "Lord, I pray, open his eyes that he may see" (v. 17).

What a dumb prayer. What a stupid prayer. The prophet has flipped out. What kind of ignorant prayer is that? Open his eyes? His eyes were already open! What scared the poor man silly is what he saw with his eyes open. And now the prophet is saying, *"Open his eyes that he may see."*

I told you that man is a spirit. The real you lives on the inside of this physical, three-dimensional body. He is in here on the inside of this physical body looking out through these windows, the eyes. When the prophet prayed and said, "Open his eyes," he was not talking about the eyes of his cranial cavity, he was talking about the eyes of his spirit. He was talking about the eyes of that man on the inside.

Look at verse 17 again: ..."**Open his eyes that he may see." Then the Lord opened the eyes of the young man, and he saw. And behold, the mountain was full of horses and chariots of fire all around Elisha.**

Glory to God! That is why he could say, "There are more with us than are with them." Here is the point of the story: when the Bible says that God opened the eyes of the young man, what did he see? Horses and chariots of fire. *They had to already be in existence.* If they were not already there, before he saw them there, even when his eyes were opened, he would not have been able to see them.

Even when you cannot see them, those angels are out there. They are there right now to protect you, and to fight for you. But you have to, by faith, believe it. You have to call them into battle, on your behalf. They are already there.

Open their eyes, Lord, that they may see. Open this reader's eyes that he may see into that spirit world by faith. Everything that God says in His Word is out there in that spirit world, but you will never see it in the physical unless you learn how to see it by faith.

19
The Prayer of Faith

Mark 11:24 would be an example of what is called *the prayer of faith*. I mentioned before that there are different kinds of prayer: the prayer of praise and worship; the prayer of agreement, where two or more are agreed together; the prayer of binding and loosing; the prayer of intercession; and the prayer of faith, or petition prayer.

Petition prayer, the most common kind of prayer, is where individuals ask the Father to do something for them or to give them something. There are parameters or laws that govern its operation, and if we do not operate according to the laws that govern it, it will not work. We are going to talk about how to put your faith into operation through the prayer of faith, or petition prayer.

The Key That Unlocks All Doors

Mark 11:24:

Therefore I say to you, whatever things you ask when you pray, believe that you receive them, and you will have them.

That statement is one of the most important statements in the Bible. It is a statement that could be the solution to any and every challenge or problem that you may ever face in life as a Christian. Mark 11:24 is the key that unlocks the door. This is the prayer of faith. This is petition prayer, and your faith is released through prayer.

Notice who is speaking in this verse. It is none other than Jesus the Christ, Messiah, the Anointed of God, the second person of the Godhead—the Son of God! The Savior, Lord, Redeemer. In common street talk, "This is the Man talking."

Faith Brings the Things You Desire

He says, **Therefore I say to you, whatever things....** Underline that word *things*. **Whatever things....** Not whatever *spirituals*, but **whatever things**. I like what the *King James Version* says in this verse:

> **Therefore I say unto you, What things soever ye desire....**

I want to stop right there, because this is and has been for many people, a tremendous stumbling block. I remember when I first got saved, and I came in contact with the church. As a youngster I was not brought up in church. I did not go to church as a child. Up till the time I was married, I never went to church, nor did I know anything about church.

When I was saved in a tent revival meeting, I was encouraged to go to a local church. So my wife and I joined a church. I was not there very long before I began to realize that Christians, based upon what I observed and heard, were not supposed to have desires of their own.

They were supposed to say, "Thy will be done," or "If it be thy will." In other words, personally as a Christian, I was not supposed to desire things for myself, but only desire what God wanted me to have. Jesus said, **What things soever ye desire...**(KJV). Now *ye* is old English for **you**. So we could say it in modern English, "Therefore I say unto *you*, what things soever *you* desire...." I want you to notice whose desire is being considered here. Not God's! Notice what it does not say, "What things soever God desires for you." But it does say, "What things soever you desire."

We are not talking about God's desires. We are not talking about God's will. We are talking about your desire and your will. It says to me that God wants me to have my desires. Since the Bible says in the mouth of two or three witnesses let every word be established, let me give you two more witnesses to confirm the fact that God wants you to have your desire.

Psalm 37:4:

Delight yourself also in the Lord, and He shall give you the desires of your heart.

Whose desire? The desire of *your* heart. Can you agree with that? Your desires. Not God's desire *for* you—*your* desires. But notice the qualifier, *delight yourself also in the Lord*. Notice that comes before the desire. **Delight yourself also in the Lord, and He shall....** But He shall not, until after you delight yourself in Him.

Delight Yourself in God's Word

What does that mean? To delight yourself in the Lord means to delight yourself in His Word. It is obvious that you do not see God standing beside you. Right? Physically, you do not see God, do you? You cannot delight yourself in someone you cannot see, or contact with your senses, but you have God present in His Word.

To delight yourself in the Lord is to delight yourself in His Word, because God and His Word are one. Now we will look at John 15:7. Jesus is speaking. He says, **If you abide....** That is the fine print in the contract. Underline or circle the word *if*. That is a very important word. A small word—only two letters, but extremely important. He says, **If you abide in Me, and My words abide in you, you will ask what you desire....** Not what God desires for you, but you will ask what *you* desire.

This is awesome. Notice, *you will* ask what you desire, and it just might, maybe, could be done for you. No! He said, **It shall be done for you.** But that is *if you abide in Me,* plus *and My Words abide in you, then you will ask what you desire*. Not what God desires, but what *you* desire.

Jesus said, **It shall be done for you**. So, I do not have to say, "If it be Thy will." That is unscriptural. "If it be Thy will?" He said, "It shall be done for you."

Let me give you the Frederick K.C. Price paraphrase of this word *abide*, because it is a very pregnant word— *pregnant* meaning it is full of many facets of revelation. Now that word *abide*, in the Greek, literally means, *to live in, settle down in, and take up residence in*.

That is a powerful definition. To live in, settle down in, and take up residence in. That means stay a while. Can you agree with that? Now watch the impact that it makes when you read it like that. **If you abide in, (live in, settle down in, and take up residence in) Me, and My words abide in (live in, settle down in and take up residence in) you, you will ask what you desire, and it shall be done for you**.

Now we can get a glimpse, to some degree, of why some of those things that you desire have not come to pass. You are not living in, settling down in, and taking up residence in His Word. And His Word has not and is not living in, settling down in, and taking up residence in you. That means it has to be with you all the time. Every day, every hour, every minute and every second, all the time.

God Wants You to Have Your Desires

The Bible says that Jesus is the truth, not a liar, so it has to come to pass. If it does not come to pass, we are the ones missing it. God cannot miss it. We are missing something. We may not intend to miss it, but we are missing it somewhere if it does not work.

I am convinced from these three passages of scriptures— Psalm 37:4, Mark 11:25 and John 15:7—that God wants me to have my desires. He might not want you to have yours.

But He wants Fred to have his. He is definitely talking to me. I believe it. I have swallowed it, hook, line and sinker, the fishing pole, the reel, the fisherman, and his boots. I have swallowed the whole thing.

I am addicted to God's Word. I am a junky on the Word of God. I have a habit of the Word of God. I have a monkey on my back called the Word of God. I have a gorilla, and I do not want him off. Now let us go back to Mark 11. You should be convinced by the Bible that God wants you to have your desires. Or, if nothing else, if you cannot bring yourself to believe that, then you say, "I know God wants Fred Price to have his desires. I know God wants Dr. Price to have his desires."

If you cannot say it for you, say it for me. Get into agreement with me, because He wants me to have my desires. Jesus said, **Therefore I say unto you, what things soever ye desire....** Then here comes the doubt peddlers and they say, "But Brother Price, dear, dear, dear Brother Price, are you implying that God would allow us to have our desires even if those desires were to be contrary to God's Word?" *I never said that!*

How Can You Know You Are in God's Will?

"Well then, Brother Price, let me ask you my second question. How can a person know whether or not this is good for him or bad for him, or if it would be something that would take him away from the things of God, or bring him to the things of God?"

That is easy! Let me ask you a question. "Why on God's green earth would you ever desire something that you do not know if it is good or bad?" Here is a good illustration. You have to use your imagination.

I have in my hand two glasses. They are the same size, made by the same company. Inside each glass is a white substance. I say to you, "I want to invite you to come and drink from my glasses. In one glass is grade A, pasteurized, homogenized milk. In the other glass is the highest grade of arsenic." Which glass would you drink from? What? Neither one! You mean to tell me you would sit there and refuse my hospitality? Tell me why you would not drink from my glasses?

You say you would not drink because you do not know which is which. In essence then, you do not know which one has the milk and which one has the arsenic? Exactly! You would be a fool to drink from either one of them if you did not know which one is the right one.

That is why God is giving you the Carte Blanche, Master Charge, American Express, Diner's Club opportunity with His Word. He has given you that thing up on your shoulders, called a brain. All you have to do is use it. It does not take very long to find out whether something is detrimental to you or not. If you do not know, why would you want it?

That is just as stupid and dumb as me going down to the local pet shop to buy my little girl a birthday present. She has this thing about kittens. She wants a little kitty cat of her own, that she can raise and cuddle and take care of. So I go down to the local pet store, walk through the door, and on one side of the wall are all these cages. Inside these cages are all these beautiful little animals, and they all look like kitty cats. They all look like little kittens.

Friend, I have news for you. If you cannot tell the difference between any alley cat cub and a lion cub, buy a dog because when that thing grows up, it may eat you. Are you getting my point? I want you to get this, because people are missing it right here.

His Word Is His Will

God is giving you credit for having enough sense to know that if you are doing what His Word says, you would never want anything that would go against His Word. The whole point is that if you are living in, and abiding in, and settling down in, and taking up residence in His Word, and His Word is abiding in, living in, settling down in, and taking up residence in you, you will *know* what is right and what is wrong. You will *know* what is good and what is bad.

That is why He can afford to say, **What things soever you desire**. He gave you His Word—all you have to do is read it. So He wants you to have your desires. I like to say it this way: "What things soever you desire that are constant with a godly life." That is as simple as I can make it.

Therefore I say unto you, what things soever ye desire, when ye pray.... My desires are to be expressed in the context of prayer. Talking to God, in other words. That may leave many out, because they do not pray. He said, **What things soever ye desire when ye pray...**(KJV). Now notice very, very carefully. It does not say, *before* you pray. It does not say *after* you pray. It says *when* you pray.

Now, when would, *when you pray* be, in point of time? *Now!* Present tense. That is what Hebrews 11:1 says: *Now* **faith is**. It does not say, "Yesterday faith was." It is always present tense. Jesus is saying the same thing that Hebrews 11:1 said. He said, **When you pray**.

He did not say, "After you pray." He could have said, "What things soever ye desire when ye see something." Or, "What things soever ye desire when ye understand something." No! He said, **What things soever ye desire, when ye pray....**

Faith Is Released Through Prayer

I know that my desire is to be couched in my prayer. We could say it like this: "Faith is released through prayer." He said, **What things soever ye (you) desire when ye (you) pray, believe....** Believe what? "Well, Brother Price, praise God, I believe. I believe that God is."

"I believe that in the beginning God created the heavens and the earth. I believe that Jesus is coming back again. I believe that after three days Jesus rose triumphant from the grave. Hallelujah."

All those things are wonderful, and you should believe all those things, but not when you pray the prayer of faith. This is not what He said to believe. He said, "When you pray, believe that you receive them, and you will have them." I have a question. What did Jesus say you are going to *have*? You say, "My desires." That is not what He said!

This is where people are missing it. People get hung up on the desires. That is not the issue. The desires are merely the focus. The issue is how to get that desire manifested in your life. Because it does not make any difference what the desire is, the modus operandi to get it manifested is going to be the same. Whether it is a car, a boat, yacht, house, clothing, food, shelter, rent payment, job, whatever, the modus operandi will be the same in every case.

You see, two and two is four. If I buy oranges, two and two is four. If I buy apples, two and two is four. If I buy airplanes, two and two is four. If I buy yachts, two and two is four, because that is a principle and the principle never changes.

The principle in faith is, when you pray, believe that you receive *them*, and you will have *them*. So, what did Jesus say you are going to have? Here is where people miss it. Notice this very carefully. He said, **Therefore I say unto you, What things soever ye desire, when ye pray, believe that ye receive them...** (KJV).

Let me say it again, we get fixated and focused on the desires. That is not the issue. Here is what He said. **Therefore I say unto you, What things soever ye desire when ye pray, believe that ye receive *them*....** Then He goes on to say, **...and ye shall have *them*** (KJV).

224

Understand that *receive them* is present tense and *will have them* is future tense. The only things that you are going to have are *them* things that you believed that you received when you prayed. If you did not believe you received anything when you prayed, guess what? You are not going to get anything.

How To Tell When You Have Believed

Here is how you can tell when you have believed that you have received them. If you prayed and believed you received them, you can never pray the second time for them. Because if you pray the second time, you are saying by your praying the second time, that you did not believe that you received them the first time, and that cancels out the prayer.

It short circuits the system. It cannot possibly work. Every time you pray for the same thing again, and ask God for it, you have canceled out the previous prayer. You are back at square one every time. Some people go through their whole life on square one, and never advance any further than that, because they do not believe they receive anything since they are still asking for it. You can only pray *once* and be in faith.

If you believed you received it, the transaction is over. You cannot pray for it again. If you pray the second time, you are saying you did not believe you received it the first time, right? Because if you believed you received it the first time, what need would there be to pray the second, third, fourth, fifth, sixtieth, ninetieth, hundredth time?

God Doesn't Respond to Begging

What we have been lead to believe, traditionally, is that if you just keep bugging God long enough, He will finally get tired of you asking and give it to you. It is like some of you with your kids. Little Johnny runs in from playing, and says, "Mommy, may I have some cookies? May I have some cookies?" And you say, "No honey, if you eat the cookies now, it will spoil your appetite." Three minutes later, "Mommy, please may I have some cookies. May I have some cookies?" You say, "No honey, I told you, you cannot have any cookies. We are going to have dinner in a little while, it will spoil your appetite."

He comes back several more times with the same request. Finally in desperation, instead of being the parent that you ought to be and taking charge over that three-year old child, you capitulate and give into the child. You give the child the cookies and say, "Here, get out of here and don't bother me anymore."

We think God is going to do that with us. He is not going to do it. God does not work that way. He is not that kind of parent who is intimidated by his kids, like some of you. You just give into the kid to get rid of him and to silence him. That is not taking control. That is not being the parent you ought to be. You told that child "no," and that is it. Signed, sealed, delivered, that is it.

Now notice again, He says, **Therefore I say to you, whatever things you ask when you pray, believe that you receive them, and you will have them.** The only things you are going to have is what you believed that you received when you prayed. If you did not believe you received anything, you are not going to have anything.

PART VI

PRACTICAL FAITH EXERCISES

20
You Can Change Your Level of Faith

Mark 11:24:

> **Therefore I say to you, whatever things you ask when you pray, believe that you receive them, and you will have them.**

There are two things that impact *when* the **you will have them** will come. The first is the nature of the thing that you are believing for, and the second is the level of your faith at the time you pray. The reason I say this is because the Bible very clearly shows us that faith can be at a greater or lesser degree of manifestation at any given point in time.

For example, in Matthew 8:5-13, the nobleman sent some people to Jesus and asked Him to come and heal his servant because he was at the point of death. Jesus started out and then the man sent another entourage to Jesus and said, "Look, Master, do not bother to come to my house. I am a man under authority. I have soldiers under me, and I tell one to go and he goes. I tell another to come and he comes, and so all You have to do is speak the word and my servant shall be healed."

Jesus turned around and looked at the crowd and said, I **have not found such great faith, not even in Israel**. The word *great* is a descriptive term. It describes a degree, a quantity, a condition or an amount. Great faith.

Little Faith Can Become Great Faith

On another occasion Jesus sent the disciples across the Sea of Galilee. He went up into a mountain to pray. After He had finished praying He came down from the mountain, and walked on the water to go to them. (Matt. 14:22-32.)

This was early in the morning. They saw Him walking on the water, and assumed, "This has to be a spirit. This cannot be a flesh and blood physical body, because flesh and blood physical bodies cannot stand on water like that—they go under. It has to be a spirit."

Jesus said, "Fear not, be of good cheer, it is I. Be not afraid." Peter said, "Lord, if it is You, let me come to You on the water." Peter got out of the boat and walked on the water to go to Jesus. But, when he saw the wind boisterous and beginning to sink, he cried out saying, "Lord, save me." Jesus reached out and caught him and said, **O you of little faith, why did you doubt?** (v. 31).

The term *little* would never be confused with the term great, and the term *great* would never be confused with the term little. They are descriptive terms of degrees, quantities, amounts or conditions.

If something could be little, it could be great. If something could be great, it could be little. There is a big difference between great and little. Faith can be at a greater or lesser degree of manifestation. That is what I meant by, *it depends on the level of your faith.*

If you have been walking by faith for two weeks, there is no way your level of faith could be as high as someone who has been consistently walking by faith for two years. It will not be the same, anymore than a twenty-three day old baby could have the same kind of physical abilities, strength and agility that a twenty-three-year-old person could have.

Let the baby that is twenty-three days old grow to twenty-three years old, and he will probably have the strength of a twenty-three year old. But he will not have the twenty-three-year-old strength when he is twenty-three days old.

If the baby tried to do, physically, what the twenty-three year old could do, he might break his back, break his arm, become completely and totally demoralized and discouraged forever and never try again, because it did not work. It is the same with faith. Your faith has to be developed. And it is developed by using it, over the years, consistently.

Many of you only use your faith like a spare tire. You never think about faith until one of the four goes flat. Then you go to the trunk to get the spare. And many times the air is out of it, because you have not taken care of it. Right? But faith is something you should be riding on all the time. So again, the level of your faith and the nature of that which you are believing God for, will determine when the, *And you will have them*, will come.

You could have a desire for something that is bigger than your faith can handle at the time. Let me give you an illustration. If you weigh 100 pounds and tried to move or push an object across the floor that weighed 400 pounds, you could not do it. The sheer weight of the 400-pound object would be too much for your 100 pounds to handle. It is possible that you could injure yourself—strain your back (your faith), or pull a muscle (your faith) and become hopelessly discouraged.

But if you, weighing 100 pounds, tried to push a 50-pound object across the floor, you would have no problem at all. Here is my point. I can have a desire, but my desire can be bigger than my faith's ability (physical strength) to move that object.

Take that over into the realm of the spiritual. It is not God, it is your faith that does it. But if you are trying to apply a hundred pounds of faith against a 400-pound desire, it is not going to compute. It will not work. So you want to use your faith on 50-pound objects—something that you can handle. And if you keep on pushing, you will finally be able to push 100 pounds, 200 pounds, 300 pounds, etc. You will progressively build up your muscles and your strength (your faith).

I said that God is not the One Who actually moves the objects or answers your prayer. Yet He is, by virtue of the fact that He has made provisions for all of the things that you need or desire that are consistent with a godly life. They are already in the earth realm. It is your faith that makes the transfer.

Let me show you a passage of Scripture that will illustrate what I am talking about. This is so important. You see, if I kept trying to move the 400-pound object, I would finally become so discouraged, so pooped out, so tired, whipped and defeated, I would probably give up. But if I could move a 50-pound object and keep on moving it, I would be encouraged by the fact that I had made some progress.

What happens is, we wait until we have a desire, like being healed, let us say from cancer or some terminal condition. And we have never even used our faith on a cold or a runny nose. We wait till we get something that is so big our faith cannot handle it. We need to use our faith on issues in life that are not necessarily 400-pound items, so that we can build our faith up to the point where we have the kind of strength (faith) to be able to move 400-pound objects. Because it is your faith that is going to do it, not God.

Mark 5:25-34:

Now a certain woman had a flow of blood for twelve years, and had suffered many things from many

physicians. She had spent all that she had and was no better, but rather grew worse. When she heard about Jesus, she came behind Him in the crowd and touched His garment. For she said, "If only I may touch His clothes, I shall be made well."

Immediately the fountain of her blood was dried up, and she felt in her body that she was healed of the affliction. And Jesus, immediately knowing in Himself that power had gone out of Him, turned around in the crowd and said, "Who touched My clothes?"

But His disciples said to Him, "You see the multitude thronging You, and You say, 'Who touched Me?'"

And He looked around to see her who had done this thing. But the woman, fearing and trembling, knowing what had happened to her, came and fell down before Him and told Him the whole truth. And He said to her, "Daughter, your faith has made you well. Go in peace, and be healed of your affliction."

Now notice it says in verse 30, **And Jesus, immediately knowing in Himself that power had gone out of Him....** Then it said in verse 29: **Immediately the fountain of her blood was dried up, and she felt in her body that she was healed of the affliction.** So something went out of Jesus, and the woman felt it. It was tangible, and she felt that healing power.

It was the power that healed her. We know that! Jesus was anointed with that power, so we could say it was Jesus who healed her.

That power was made available because of Jehovah Rapha—**For I am the Lord who heals you** (Exodus 15:26). We could say it was God Almighty who healed her. We could say it was Jesus. We could say it was the power or the anointing. But it is interesting that Jesus gave neither Himself, nor His Father, nor the power, the credit for healing the woman.

And He said to her, "Daughter, your faith has made you well." He said her faith did it. But it could not have done it, if that power was not available. That power is available today for you and for me. That power is available, but it takes our faith to release or activate the power. The very fact that she touched Him, (and she did it by an exercise of her faith), that power was released to heal her.

Suppose she had never come in contact with the power? Suppose she had never touched Him? Obviously, for the first twelve years she was not healed. So we could not say that because she was not healed that it was not God's will. We could not say that. And yet that is what some would dare to say. "Well, it is not God's will." No! No!

The proper ingredients have to be brought together, and the principles have to be operated in order for the power of God, which is present all the time, everywhere, to be activated. The power has to be accessed and activated, and it takes our faith to do it. Not God! All you have to do is use your head. Just use a little deductive reasoning. If it were God Who overtly reached out and did the healing, then every person that God touched would be healed the same way, in the same amount of time. It would not make any difference what the condition was—God's power is omnipotent power.

If God was automatically doing it on His own, anyone who God touched would be healed the same way. But why do things work differently? Some people's healing is instantaneously manifested. Others, it takes a process of time before it comes into manifestation. Why? Because it is the faith of the people. It is not God. The power is already here, but you have to release that power to the issues of your life in order for it to do you any good. Do you understand that? It is up to you!

Use Your Faith on the Little Things

Use your faith on the little things—things that do not make any difference if they do not come to pass. For instance, if you get a headache, the most natural thing to do is get an aspirin. There is nothing wrong with that. But I would encourage you not to take the aspirin. Instead, use your faith.

I say use your faith, because usually headaches are not terminal conditions. Use your faith on something that is not life threatening, so that if it does not come to pass, you will not die. You may go through some pain, but pain is not dying, because you can die without any pain. What you want to do is use your faith on little things that are non-consequential—things that are not life threatening until you develop your faith so that if a big thing does come, then you will be able to handle it. Your faith will have been developed to where you can stand against it.

You are not perfect and sometimes you do some dumb things without realizing they are dumb. You do things that give Satan a license to have an access door into your circumstances to destroy you. And sometimes it is not until you get in it that you find out what you have done wrong. If you do not have enough faith and enough power going for you to ward off the attack until something can be done about the condition, you could die.

The cancer attack on my wife is a perfect example. Because she used her faith all the time, her faith was strong. Her Word knowledge was strong. So when she found out that the situation was there, she applied her faith to it and through that means, with the help of the doctors, the cancer was eradicated.

But most of the time people end up dying. The reason they do is because their faith level is so low. You have to use your faith on little things, then when the big things do occur, if they do come—and the enemy will bring some things against you—then you will be able to stand against it.

I told you there were two things that determine how long it will take for, *And you will have them*, to come to pass. I want to make point 2A and also say this, that in the process of, *And you will have them*, you also have an adversary who seeks whom he may destroy. He is the thief—Satan—who comes to steal, kill and destroy. He is going to come against you in that interim period.

When I make my confession of faith, and say, "I believe I have received," all the time that I am making that confession, Satan in the spirit world is coming against my mind, against my circumstances, against my body.

You Must Stand Against the Enemy

I have to be able to *stand*. Not just to believe that I have received, but also to stand against the onslaught of the enemy who will surely come. He will come primarily against your mind.

His first and primary attack will be in reference to fear. He will try to bring fear. "What is going to happen if? Suppose they do not get it all? Suppose it is too late? Suppose it is inoperable? The doctor has already told you, there is nothing they can do."

Fear kills most people, not the sickness and disease. Because what fear will do is cause you to do some irrational things. It makes you do some things that you would not ordinarily have done if you were not scared. So you have to have enough faith in operation so that when the fear comes, you will not only believe you have received and make that confession, but you will stand against this onslaught of the enemy trying to beat you to death with fear.

You Are in a War

During the time of exercising your faith on an issue that your faith can handle, and based upon your level of faith, you also have to contend with the enemy coming against you. You are in a warfare.

He does not want you to get it, so he will come against you. He will come through your friends, through your relatives, through the circumstances—all kinds of ways. "O, you don't look too good. Are you sure you are all right? Are you sure that faith stuff's going to work? You know so-and-so had that same thing and they died. Brother are you sure? I know three people who had the same thing and they foreclosed on their homes. They lost their homes."

The confession, "I believe I have received," has to be kept in the present tense. Even though it is ten days after you prayed, your confession has to be, "I believe I am." Not going to get healed. Not being healed. "*I am healed.*"

Confession Is Always Present Tense

Even though the manifestation may come progressively, and you don't see yourself getting better, your confession has to be, "I believe I am." Present tense. "I believe *I am*. I believe my need *is met*. I believe my taxes *are paid*." Whatever it is, "I believe that it is so." Do you understand that"? This is where the battle is won or lost!

You may say, "That does not make sense." You are right, it does not make sense, because we are not dealing with sense, we are dealing with faith. That is exactly the point, it does not make sense. But you do not have anything to lose but your problem.

You have done a lot of other crazy things that did not make sense. Someone told you, "Do not do that, it is foolish," and you did it anyway. Why not do this? You have nothing to lose but your problem. Because even if it did not work, what is the difference, you are going to die anyway. Go for it! Go ahead and stand on the Word of God. It just might be that your faith is stronger than you realize that it is and can make the difference between whether the devil takes you out or not.

Use Common Sense

Do not wait until you have a terminal condition or a situation where they are ready to foreclose. Do not wait until you have missed twelve payments and they are ready to foreclose on your house. Believe God for the payments in the first place. And do not try to bite off more than your faith can handle. Use some common sense.

Just because you have a desire for a thing does not mean you have the faith to cause that thing to come to pass. Remember, it is your faith that is going to bring it to pass. Jesus said, **Daughter, your faith has made you well.**

We know it was God's power, but it was her faith that released the power necessary to bring her healing. It was not God and yet it was God, in that God provided it. It is the same with you. He has already provided it. It is already here. Basically, everything you need and everything that you would ever desire that is consistent with a godly life, is already here in the earth realm. God does not have to send it down from heaven as an afterthought—it is already here. But it is our faith that brings it to us.

Use Your Faith for Finances

Faith can work in several different ways. It can work progressively—over time. That is why I encourage people to use faith on things that are non-life threatening. For instance, if you have credit or a charge card, the easiest thing in the world is to go charge something.

The next time you need something, instead of charging it, use your faith. Now I am talking about when you are just starting out to learn how to develop your faith. There is nothing wrong with a charge card and nothing wrong with using it, but it does not take any faith as such, to use a charge card.

It may take some faith to pay the bill when it comes in thirty days. It may take a whole lot of faith and a whole lot of money. But what I am saying is, believe God for it, that the power of God will supernaturally produce it, rather than having to use the charge card.

Start believing God for pantyhose, or you will never believe for a designer suit. If your faith will not work to produce six dollar pantyhose, how are you going to get a designer suit for a thousand dollars? Start believing for pantyhose because that is not like life and death. Another example, use your faith on making payments. If you cannot make a payment for three hundred dollars a month, how are you going to believe God for an automobile that costs $25,000 in one lump sum?

We started out using our faith on making payments. Now I do not tell my business just to be telling it or to show off or brag about it. But just like the illustrations I use, I want you to get the point, and I am willing to expose myself if that is what it takes.

I want you to see that it works. It is not theoretical. These are actual things that are happening, not to someone you read about, that lived three-hundred years ago. Those stories are wonderful and I can gain great inspiration from them, but I can gain more inspiration from someone I can actually see and touch and know that they have to know what I am going through, because they are living under the same tax structure that I am. They are breathing the same polluted air that I am breathing, and they are in the same country that I am in.

We started believing God for a hundred and fifty-five dollar a month payment on a car. For us at that time it was the biggest payment we had ever made. In fact that payment, at that time, was bigger than the house payment—$155 a month. Big deal. But that is what it was at that time. Everything is relative.

We started using our faith to believe for that car. My wife was the instigator of it. She was the one who said, "We are going to buy a new car." And like all hard-headed men, I wanted a new car and that was all the excuse I needed. My wife said it. "We are going to get a new car." We men usually just go out and buy one. If our wives like it, fine. If they do not like it, fine. We bring it home. "Honey, I bought a new car."

So we started using our faith and that was the easiest thing we ever believed for. We were able to believe the money in over and above our paycheck. Now after using our faith for a number of years, I was able to go in and buy a car and write the man a check for $60,000 cash. I paid cash for the car. But I did not start there, at $60,000. I started at $155 a month.

We got that $155 working regularly, then we went on to two-hundred, three-hundred, four-hundred, five-hundred, over time. Finally, we made it to the point where our faith had produced to such an extent that we did not have to believe for the payment. I just went in and told the man, "I want one of those. I want it that color." I custom ordered it.

When the car came in, he called me and said, "It is $60,000." I said, "Fine, I will be right down." I went down, whipped out my checkbook, whipped out my pen, wrote out a check, gave him the check, got the keys to the car, got in the car, made no payments, drove it home and gave it to my wife.

21
Don't Try To Believe
Beyond Your Measure of Faith

Learn how to believe God for the little things. Do not try to believe beyond your measure of faith at its present state of development. When I say, "Do not try to use your faith on something that is bigger than your faith can handle," I do not mean to say, "Do not use your faith." But you need to understand that if you are in a terminal situation—if your situation is a one thousand dollar problem—you would need one thousand dollars to eradicate that problem. If you only have one dollar, it is not going to work. You will have to increase that dollar to the one thousand dollar level.

Let us say that, all of a sudden you start having pain— and that is what can happen, especially with things like sickness and disease. You can have something growing inside of your body, and not even know it at first, and the thing can get a head start on you. By the time you feel some pain and realize that something is wrong, you go to the doctor and have a checkup, and he tells you, "You have a grapefruit-size tumor and we give you nine months to live."

What I am saying is, your one dollar faith is not going to work on that. Do not try to use your faith on that and die in the process. That is what I want to get across to you. You may need some help. Some doctor help. Some medical help. Some surgery help. Some treatment help. Do not try to use your one dollar faith on a situation that is terminal. *I am not saying do not use it.* You *can* apply your faith to it, but you need *more* than that one dollar faith at that point.

You cannot afford to sit around waiting, saying, "I believe that I am healed," and you only have one dollar faith in operation, because that thing could kill you. At that point, you may need some help to get rid of that condition, like an operation. And that is not in contradiction to faith. God wants you well. That is why He invented doctors to help us.

Sometimes when we find out about things, we did not know that something was wrong with us. And most people never think about their faith until they get a flat tire. Just like the spare. You never think about the spare tire until you get a flat. But I guarantee you one thing, if you go outside to where your car is parked and one of those four is flat, the first thing you think about is not your mama, not your papa, not the goose, not the duck, not the dog, but you think, *spare tire*. If you do not know where it is and how to use it, you could still be in trouble.

Don't Wait for a Crisis To Exercise Faith

That is what is happening to many of you concerning your faith. You do not use your faith until you get in a crisis, such as a tumor or a diagnosis of six months to live, and then you only have one dollar faith in operation, because you have never really used it.

You have used your own ability, your own smarts, and now here comes a terminal condition. That is what I meant by, do not try to use your faith on that. It is not going to work. You may die. That is why I say, use your faith on something that is small that you can handle. If it does not come to pass within a given amount of time, it is not going to kill you.

You can use your faith to believe that God will help you through the doctor. Take that one dollar faith and apply it to the surgery or to the treatment. God wants you alive. He does not want you dead. He gets no joy and no glory out of you as His child, dying.

Doctors Are Instruments of God

I need to say this, because some people have the strange idea that to walk by faith means you do not believe in going to doctors or use operations or treatments. These types will brand me as a heretic for what I just said, or they will brand me as someone who really does not believe in the message of faith, because I advocate going to the doctor.

But remember that doctors, medicine, and treatments are not opposed to God. They are not trying to kill you. Doctors are trying to help you, because God invented doctors. I told you this before. God is the One Who instituted medicine, not the devil. Satan was not the one who instituted medical help, because it would be to his advantage for there to be no doctors. And as a result, most people would die—especially most Christians—because they do not know much about faith.

Faith Is Progressive

Understand this, faith is progressive. I say it again, do not wait until you have a terminal situation. It could be a foreclosure on your house. That is terminal. It could be something physical in your body. That is still terminal. So, use your faith now, while you have situations that are not life and death situations.

I said this before, if you get a headache, do not take an aspirin. Now if you do not listen to what I am saying, it might sound like a contradiction. I just said, "Go to the doctor," "Have an operation." Now I am saying, "Do not take an aspirin for a headache." No! I am not saying that. What I am saying is, headaches are not usually terminal conditions. People do not usually die from headaches. So if you don't get a headache healed supernaturally, it does not matter, because you can always resort to a pill like an aspirin.

But here is an excellent place to start using your faith. If you cannot believe God to get rid of a headache or whatever causes a headache, how are you going to believe for a grapefruit-sized tumor to disappear? If you cannot get rid of headaches, how are you going to get rid of tumors? It will take more faith to get rid of a grapefruit-sized tumor than it will for you to get rid of the headache. That is why I say, "Do not take the pill," because it is always available. But start taking a stand and using your faith on the little things like a headache.

Get headaches to go away regularly, and then you may be able to forestall anything bigger than a headache that may come upon you. Or if, by chance, you find that it has come upon you, because of something you were doing and did not know you were doing it, that was contributing to Satan having an opportunity to put that on you, you will be able to stand against it.

I gave you an illustration of an automobile. I used the purchase of a car, and I talked about the monthly payment. Once we found out how to walk by faith, we started using our faith just to make payments. If you cannot make a payment regularly with your faith, how are you going to buy something and pay cash for it? In other words, if you cannot make a hundred and fifty-five dollar-a-month payment with your faith, supernaturally believing that money in over and above your regular expenses, how are you going to believe for a fifty-thousand dollar automobile for cash? It is a lot easier to believe for a hundred and fifty-five dollar a month payment, than it is to believe for fifty thousand cash. That is my point.

As I said before, it is not God Who is going to answer that prayer. It is not God, and yet it is God. It is not God in that He is just going to reach down to earth, *zappo* and answer the prayer. But it is God in that He has provided all that is necessary for the prayer to be answered.

It is already in the physical earth realm. What is going to do it is your faith. I gave you the illustration from Mark, chapter 5 about the woman with the issue of blood. The Bible said that power went out of Jesus. We know that it was the power that healed her, but Jesus never gave credit to the power. He never gave credit to Himself as Messiah. He never gave credit to Jehovah Rapha, the Lord Who heals. But He said, "Daughter, your faith has made you well."

Yet we know it was God, in that God provided the power. But if she had had no faith in operation to activate that power, even though the power was available, it would not have done her any good. It takes *our* faith and *God's* power to produce the deliverance. Do you understand that? God's power is present all the time, everywhere, twenty-four hours a day, but it takes our faith to activate that power in our circumstances.

Start using your faith on little things. We had bought a car and we were making a payment on the car of a hundred and fifty-five dollars a months. Remember, everything is relative. For us at that time it was the biggest payment we had ever made on anything. It was even bigger than the house payment we were making at that time. But my wife and I got into agreement and we started using our faith to believe God for the money to come in.

That car was the easiest thing that we ever paid for, because the money supernaturally came in over and above our regular, weekly paycheck. The paycheck was not enough as it was. So we believed the Word of God, and our faith moved in the realm of finances and brought that money to us.

I jumped from that one, then told you that later on I bought a car for my wife and paid sixty-thousand dollars for it. I think you would agree that there is a difference between $155 a month and $60,000 cash. I want to be sure you understand the step-by-step progression. That is too big of a jump from $155 to $60,000. It is not going to work that way for you and it did not for us.

Faith Grows in Steps

Actually, it takes intermittent steps to get there. We walked these steps. After we paid for the car (which by the way, we paid off a couple of years ahead of time), then the next financial thing that I applied my faith to was a car I bought my wife, and for the first time paid cash for it.

I bought her a Toyota Corolla for four-thousand dollars cash. It was a big step from $155 to $4,000. That is where our faith was, and I believed God for that $4,000 to come in. It came in, I put it in the bank, and then bought my wife her first car for $4,000. The steps kept going on.

I am using financial things for illustration because that is something you can see. It is something you can relate to, but the principle works the same for everything. It does not matter what it is. It works the same way, but it is progressive. That is what I want you to understand. Then I went from the $4,000 Toyota and decided to buy a Lincoln. At that time, 1977, the Lincoln Continental was the biggest Lincoln built. Now, they have changed that and they have the Continental, the Mark Series, and the TownCars. Now, the Lincoln Continental is a smaller car than the TownCar. But at that time, the Lincoln Continental was the biggest car that the Lincoln people made.

I wanted a Continental. That was my desire, to have a luxury car. So I believed God. I got the car on a lease. Someone had told me that a lease could save money. I leased the car and found out I still had to pay the full amount at the end of the lease if I wanted the car to be mine. It is just easier to get into it, because the downpayment is smaller. After thinking about it, I said, "This does not make sense. I'm still making payments and losing money by still having to pay interest on it."

We applied our faith to the situation. At that time, the pay-off on that car was seventeen-thousand dollars. We believed God for the money, and the money came in. We paid that car off—$17,000. Next, I wanted another Lincoln. At that time they started scaling down the big cars. The Lincoln Continental at that time was a big car. Then they started the "Mark" Series. So I bought a "Mark" Series and believed God for the money and paid twenty-five thousand dollars cash for that car. The next car that I bought was the one I bought for my wife for sixty-thousand dollars.

Then I believed God for a car that cost a hundred and twenty-five thousand dollars—a Rolls Royce. Remember Jesus said, "What things soever ye desire," and I desired a Rolls Royce. Different strokes for different folks. Some people like dogs and some people like cats, and I wanted a Rolls Royce. So I believed God for a Rolls Royce. Remember, I told you that it is your faith that does it. However, you do not know how your faith is going to produce it.

There are basically only two ways for your faith to produce something. Either you get the money and go buy it, or someone gives it to you. Either way, you get it. Someone paid the money, but it was your faith that caused the money to be paid.

I used the Rolls Royce in an illustration when we were over on Crenshaw Boulevard in the Inglewood facility to help people understand progressively how these things work. I was not trying to tell anyone my business, but I was just using it as an illustration, because I like to use real life things that people can relate to. "Mary had a little lamb" is fine, but I have never seen Mary nor the lamb. So I like to use something that people can actually see.

I made mention of the Rolls Royce, as an illustration, and God put it in the heart of someone to give me the Rolls Royce. I did not have to pay one penny for it. Why not drive a hundred and twenty five thousand dollar car if it is given to me? So do not get on my case. It surely was not Satan who gave it to me, because when I got the car I said, "Praise the Lord." I did not say, "Praise Satan." I did not say, "Halle-satan, Halle-satan, Halle-satan, Halle-satan." I said, "Hallelujah, Hallelujah, Praise the Lord." God, through my faith, gave me that car.

I am trying to show you the progressive steps: one hundred and fifty-five, four thousand, seventeen thousand, twenty-five thousand, sixty thousand, a hundred and twenty-five thousand. There is no telling where I am going next. But all I am trying to get you to see is that it is progressive. So start using your faith on things that are non-life threatening, so that if it does not come to pass, you will not die.

If you are dealing with a terminal condition or a foreclosure, do not try to use your faith on it because if you did not have enough faith to make the payments before it got into foreclosure, how do you think you are going to get out of the foreclosure now? It was easier to make the monthly payments, so that ought to tell you that your faith is not strong enough. *Get some help*, which means you might have to get a loan.

Faith Works With Credit

Some people have the idea that when you walk by faith you cannot buy anything on time or installment payments, or use credit cards or borrow money. I will borrow anything that is not nailed down to get to my objective. Sometimes that is the better part of wisdom if your faith is not up to your desire level.

Let me give you another good illustration. We paid off a house, using our faith, twenty years ahead of the mortgage. We used our faith, and believed God for not only the payments but for the extra money to pay the house off. We did not want to pay thirty years' worth of interest. So we paid that thirty-year mortgage off in ten years. Then we decided we wanted another, larger house in another area.

In the area where we lived, they did not have houses of the magnitude and size that we wanted. So we went into an area to look for a house, the kind of house we wanted. We used to drive through this area and dream. Ever lose your dream? Keep your dream. So we went through this area, and at that time we had no idea how much houses cost. We had just paid off our house and that house had cost us thirty thousand dollars when we first bought it ten years before. At today's prices, it was not all that much money, but to us, it was a lot of money.

We had not been out in the real estate market at the time and we had no idea how much houses cost. So, we were driving through this area, saw a "For Sale" sign with an open house, and said, "Well, let's go in and look at this house and see what kind of house it is."

On the outside this was the kind of house we wanted. It was a beautiful house. We walked through the house and looked at all the rooms, and said, "This is the kind of house we want. This is it, honey." So I went to the broker and asked how much the house cost. And they told me. Now remember, everything is relative. We had just finished paying off a mortgage twenty years ahead of time, which we had originally bought ten years before, for thirty thousand dollars.

This guy tells us that this house cost $90,000. Again, remember everything is relative. I said to myself, "$90,000! I cannot count that high. Ninety thousand dollars! This guy must be crazy." I am saying this to myself. We played it off like it was nothing. We went outside, got in the car and looked at each other and said, "This guy must by crazy. Ninety thousand dollars? He must be out of his mind." I never heard of anything like that in my life. That was absolutely insane. I said, "Ninety thousand dollars? No way!"

About six months later we were driving through the same area and there was another house up for sale with an open house. We went in and looked at the house. The floor plan was a little different than the first house we looked at, but basically the same size house, the same square footage. This house was one hundred thousand dollars—ninety thousand to one hundred thousand dollars in six months. Later we went and looked at another house. It was one hundred ten thousand dollars! Then another house some time later, and it was one hundred twenty thousand dollars!

Houses did not care about what I thought about how much they cost. They just kept on escalating in price. Finally, we looked at another house priced at one hundred thirty thousand dollars. Then wisdom set in. Here is where sometimes buying something on time can be directly inspired by God. We saw another house. We liked this house, but the price tag was one hundred forty thousand dollars. I began to think. I said, "Now wait a minute, this house was ninety thousand dollars. While I am fussing and arguing about how high the prices are, the houses have gone up fifty thousand dollars more than they were before. And there is no telling how much higher they are going to go."

Cash Only Is Not Always the Best Way

You see, I had made up my mind, after we paid that other house off, we were never going to make payments anymore. Not the kid! Payments? No! Cash! Oh yes, the next house I buy, cash only. Now while I am using my faith to save ninety thousand dollars, these houses have gone up to one hundred forty thousand dollars. By having to believe in another fifty thousand dollars, the house will go up to two hundred thousand. Then while I am believing for another sixty thousand to make the two hundred thousand, the house may go up to two hundred fifty thousand.

So I said, "Wait a minute. If I buy this house now, it cannot go up anymore. I can always believe to pay it off. Once I make an offer and we go into escrow and I purchase that house, I do not care what the real estate market does, *that house* cannot go up another dime." So we nailed that house down at one hundred forty thousand dollars, and then paid that sucker off in three years.

There is a place where buying something on time can be a blessing, as well as wisdom. We believed God to pay the house off ahead of time and that we would not have to pay a prepayment penalty for paying if off ahead of the thirty-year mortgage. I still saved money. I saved twenty-seven years' worth of interest. That is wisdom.

We started out believing God for $155. I have only used these personal illustrations to show you that walking by faith is progressive. So do not let anyone put you in bondage. As a church, we used the same principle when we bought the church on Crenshaw Boulevard. We bought it on time. We had a fifteen-year mortgage, and we paid it off in seven years.

During that seven years the price could not go up any higher. It would have continued to escalate in price, but we had nailed it down at $750,000. I am sure you are aware of it. Just look at our whole society. Over the years everything has gone up, up, up, up, up. And there is nothing you can do about it but pay the price. But if you buy property like that, you can nail that sucker down right now, and then believe God to pay it off.

But understand, you have to have that kind of faith. We had one hundred forty thousand dollar faith, we just did not have it in actual cash. If you only have one dollar faith, do not buy a house for one hundred forty thousand dollars, and think you are going to pay it off in three years. You are not, because your faith is not up to that level. Do you understand what I am talking about?

I am only using the house as an example to illustrate the faith principle, but the principle is the same, applied to whatever you apply it to. I use the house and the car, because it is something everyone can relate to. The houses and the cars are not the issue. The issue is the principle. Just like 2 and 2 is 4, whether you are buying oranges, apples, bananas or chitterlings. Now, we know that we have to believe we receive when we pray and then make our confession that we believe that we have received.

Don't Let Discouragement In

Let me say it again, do not try to believe for something that is so big for you, you cannot do it and become discouraged because it does not come to pass. Start using your faith on little things, things that are easy for you to believe for, so that as your faith gets stronger, your confidence level will rise correspondingly. When you get a victory, you get confidence. When you have defeats, you can become demoralized and you will stop using your faith.

That is what some have done. They tried to bite off too much and did not have the faith. They had the desire, but did not have the faith. When it did not come to pass they got discouraged. They gave it up. But if you will walk like I am telling you to, you will *never* give up. *The Word of God works!*

If everyone on this planet, and I do not care who they are, stopped believing that faith is that which moves the hand of God, I would be the only one on the planet still believing, because I have been there. I know. You cannot talk me out of it. It is too late to try to dissuade me. I have been there.

I have been down, and now I am up, and up is better. I have been sick and now I am well, and well is better. I have been poor, and now I am rich—rich meaning abundantly supplied. I am not a multi-millionaire *yet*, but rich, biblically speaking, means abundant supply. So much supply that I have enough to give away. That is what Bible *rich* means.

Do not come to me and try to float a loan, because I am not going to loan you a dime. Now you ask, "Why?" Because once I found out how to walk by faith, I never asked anyone for anything. I only asked my Father for it. The Bible told me, "My God shall supply all my needs." The Bible does not say, "Fred Price shall supply all your needs." If you come to me, I am going to say, "What did I just teach you?"

22

You Must Learn Faith for Yourself

Take it and use it just like I did. Because once you do it that way, then no one, the devil included, can ever talk you out of it. I do not care what anyone does. I know from whence I have come, so I cannot be talked out of it. I know it works. But you have to work it.

It is not going to fall on you like leaves off of a tree. It will work if you will apply the principles. And as a result, you will finally get to a point where you are free. Then and only then, you can be used as a channel of blessing.

Most people are so bound up with their own problems and with their own lack, they have nothing to give to anyone else. They need someone to give them something. But when you get to the point where you have it to give away and you can be a channel of blessing, that is when life begins to be fun—when you do not have to spend all your waking moments trying to figure out how you are going to make it, or how you are going to take care of your things, your children or your family.

Remember To Be Thankful

You can get to a point where you will be thinking about how you can give to other people. That is when it gets to be fun, fun, fun, fun, fun. Jesus said, "When you pray, believe you receive and you will have." I told you that when you pray your initial prayer of faith to believe you receive something, you need to support that prayer by a constant prayer of thanksgiving that you believe you have it. You continue to say, "Father, I thank You, I believe that I am healed." Or, "I believe that my need is met." Or, "I believe that I have that new job."

Whatever it is, you continue to support your original prayer by the prayer of thanksgiving. What that does is keep you attuned and alert to the things that you prayed for. It also lets the evil one know that you are on the job, so that his demons cannot come and try to dissuade you and discourage you by getting you to look at the circumstances and say, "Well, you see how hard it is right now, how tight it is economically. You know you are not going to get that now."

But you have to learn how to look at the Word, not at the circumstances. Remember, the scriptural principle is, "Faith comes by hearing." Every time *you* say it *you* hear it. And that will stimulate your faith. Do you understand? When you say it out loud, "Praise God, I believe my need is met," you hear that. Faith comes by hearing and it will stimulate your faith.

1 John 5:14:

> **Now this is the confidence that we have in Him, that if we ask anything according to His will, He hears us.**

What is confidence? How about assurance, guarantee or trust? Can you agree that confidence would mean trust? If I have confidence in you, I can trust you. If I do not trust you, I surely do not have any confidence in you.

Notice what it says: **Now this is the confidence that we have in Him,** (in God), **that if we ask anything....** I do not know about you, but the word *anything* sounds a lot like, "What things soever ye desire." He says, "If we ask anything according to His will." Here is the key. We have to ask according to His will. If we do, He says "He hears us."

Now think about this. *"For God to hear you, is for God to answer you."* He says, **If we ask anything according to His** will. "Yes, Brother Price, but that is my problem. I do not know what the will of God is. I do not know whether it is God's will or not." Well, that lets me know that you do not read the Bible, because if you read the Bible, God's Word, then you will know God's will.

Always remember that God's Word is God's will, and God's will is God's Word. Anything that you will ever need, or anything that you could ever desire that is consistent with a godly life, is covered in the contract, or in the covenant. *It is in there!* So what I have learned to do is, when I pray, I pray the Word. I figure there is no point in reinventing the wheel. God did an excellent job when He invented it the first time. So I just find Scripture (Bible verses) that cover my need or desire.

"Yes, but how in the world, Dr. Price, do you get a Rolls Royce out of the Bible? I have been reading the Bible and I have not seen a Rolls Royce in the Bible." That is because you have not been looking. It is in there. I tell you, Rolls Royces are in there. We just read it in Mark 11:24: **What things soever ye desire** (KJV). And then Paul said in Philippians 4:19, **My God shall supply all your need**.

I have a need for transportation. I cannot count on public transportation. I have too much to do, too many places to go. I cannot be locked into having to wait for a bus that may or may not show up, or for some folk to go on strike or not go on strike. So I have two things. I need transportation, and I agree with you, I do not need a Rolls Royce to be transported. But He did say, "What things soever I desire."

That was my desire and He gave it to me. Are you following me? So it was covered. It is in there. Houses are in there. So if I want a house up on a hill—I mean, what is the difference in a house on a hill and a house in the valley? A house in the valley I do not want. A house on the hill I do want. That is my desire, so I got a house on the hill.

That is what I wanted, a house on a hill. And God put me on a hill. I am the highest one in the area where I live. Everyone in the area has to look up to my house. I look down on everyone around me. In my immediate area, I am on the higher ground. My Father put me on higher ground. I asked for it, He gave it to me. What can I say? So it is all covered in the Word.

Ask According to His Word

Notice again, First John 5:14:

> Now this is the confidence that we have in Him, that if we ask anything according to His will, He hears us.

This Bible says that in order for God to hear me when I pray or ask, I have to ask according to His will. Now since this is God's Word, and God is the One Who made the covenant, and God is the One Who makes the requirements that I have to pray according to His will in order for Him to hear me, then God is doing that. He has obligated Himself to make His will known to me. Because if He does not provide me with His will, then I will never know whether I am asking according to His will.

Therefore, I could never have the confidence or trust that He heard me when I prayed. He obligates Himself by telling me that in order for Him to hear me, I have to ask according to His will. That means that God's will has to be available to me.

He said, **Now this is the confidence...that if we ask anything....** Brother, sister, that is awesome. **...anything according to His will, He hears us.** For God to hear is for God to answer. Now again, you have to bring everything that the Word says about a transaction to bear on the situation, even though a Scripture verse such as this one does not tell you everything else. But you have to know that.

When He said, **Now this is the confidence that we have in Him, that if we ask anything according to His will...,** *anything*. That means you also have to have faith for the *anything*. You have to have one thousand dollar faith if you want one thousand dollar anythings. You cannot have one dollar faith and expect to ask for one thousand dollar anythings. The anythings have to be consistent with your level of faith. Do you understand that?

First John 5:14 says, **Now this is the confidence that we have in Him, that if we ask anything according to His will, He hears us.** Verse 15: **And if we know that He hears us, whatever we ask, we know that we have the petitions that we have asked of Him.**

And if we.... What? Know. What? Know. "Well, I'm just hoping and praying that the Lord heard my prayer." No! No! The man said, **And if we** *know* **that He hears us.** How do we know that He hears us? Because verse 14 just got through saying, **Now this is the confidence that we have in Him, that if we ask anything according to His will, He hears us.**

I do not have to *feel* like He does, I *know* He does, because He said He does. The Bible says it is impossible for God to lie. God does not lie. So if He said He hears me, then I do not have to wonder if God heard my prayer. I know that He heard it. "That's what I don't like about that Fred Price. He's so arrogant. Who does he think he is?"

I just read it in the Word. That is not arrogance, it is confidence. God is the One Who said it, not me. **And if we know that He hears us.** I just believe God. I believe that He means what He says, and says what He means.

23
Faith Believes You Have What You Pray For

1 John 5:15:

> And if we know that He hears us, whatever we ask, we know that we have the petitions that we have asked of Him.

Notice what it does *not* say. It does not say, "And we know that we are going to get it." That would be future tense. The man said "We know that we have." "We have" is what tense—past, present or future? Present! That is why when you pray the prayer of faith, also known as petition prayer, you can only pray once and be in faith. The man told you, you already have it.

If you have it, why are you still asking for it? You have it now, by faith. Why? Because Hebrews 11:1 says that **...faith is...the evidence....** Not the thing. Faith is the evidence of the thing not perceived by your senses. So I have my faith to take the place of the thing until the thing arrives. Faith becomes the evidence. We have them by faith.

Look at it again in the *King James Version*: **...we know that we have the petitions that we desired of him.** That sounds like Mark 11:24, right? **...What things soever ye desire....** There it is, we have the petitions that we desired of Him. So if I believe that I have it, then I cannot ask for it again. Because if I ask for it again, I am saying by my asking, I must not have it. Because if I actually had it, why would I ask for it again?

What you do in support of that original prayer of faith, is to pray the prayer of thanksgiving, that you believe that you have it. Let me give you a scenario: Monday I pray and say, "Father, I believe that I receive my healing." Tuesday the healing has not manifested. I am still in pain. The knot or growth is still there, or whatever it might be. So Tuesday in my prayer time, I say, "Father, I want to thank You. I believe I received my healing on Monday. I believe I am healed."

Understand, you have to keep it in the present tense. Wednesday, it is still there. I still feel the pain, I still see the knot or lump. My prayer on that day is "Father, I thank You. I believe I received my healing on Monday. I believe I am healed." Thursday, Friday, Saturday, Sunday, the same thing. Seven days. Monday I wake up, the pain is gone the growth and knot are gone. On that day I pray and say, "Father, I thank You, *I am healed*." End of transaction. Do you understand that? Do you see how to do it? That is how it works.

Never Give Up

Sometimes whatever it is you are believing for may take longer than that. I will give you a personal experience. Years ago, and this was before I found out about how to walk by faith, I had a growth that developed in the left side of my chest cavity. It was unnatural and extremely painful.

When I first noticed it, it was like a little bump, about the size of a green pea, underneath the skin. I could feel it right under the mammary gland. I was aware of it when I showered.

Over the years, very slowly that thing grew. It got bigger, and bigger, and bigger. Finally, when I got married, it had developed to about the size of a silver dollar. It was pretty big, and very, very painful. If I was playing sports or something, and one of the guys happened to hit me in that spot, I would fall out on the ground like I had died. They thought someone shot me, because it was painful.

At that time I was in a church that did not tell me about what I am telling you in this book. I was in a church that did not tell me that God still heals. They told me that God turned all of the healing over to the doctors and that He does not heal people anymore supernaturally. And so I thanked God for doctors. I came to a point where I could not stand the pain any longer. Something had to go. Something had to give. So I went to the doctor. The doctor examined me, checked me out. He said, "Yes, Mr. Price, you have a growth there. It does not appear to be malignant, but it will constantly cause you pain. The only thing that we can do is to operate and take it out."

He drew me a little diagram and showed me how they would do it. He said, "We go in right below the mammary gland and make an incision. We lay the flesh back, reach in, take out the growth, sew it back up. For a while there will be a depressed area, a depression where we take out some of the tissue. Over a period of time the depression will fill in with fatty tissue, and it will look relatively normal. The only thing you will see will be the incision."

I said, "Well, Doc, do whatever you have to do, because I cannot stand this pain anymore." Thank God for doctors. I went to the doctor, he operated, took the growth out. I came back for my final checkup and he said, "Everything is fine. There was no malignancy. As I pointed out to you before, there will be some pain while the incision is healing up and there will be that depressed area, but over a period of time, the only thing that you will have to remind you that you had the operation will be that little scar from the incision."

So time went on. After that I found out about the reality of the Word. I got filled with the Holy Spirit and started speaking with other tongues. I began to get the revelation of the Word of God. I found out that with Jesus' stripes I was healed.

The doctor had told me when I went for my last checkup, "Mr. Price, there is a remote possibility that vestiges of this growth could still be in your blood stream, and might be carried to the other side of your chest cavity. This particular kind of growth does that sometimes. I do not know for sure if it will do that or not, but I just want you to be aware that there is a remote possibility of that."

As the years went by, I noticed one day when I was showering, a little bump under the skin. I said, "Uh oh, there it is again." Only this time this thing grew seven hundred miles an hour. This thing grew the size of a silver dollar, almost overnight it seemed. And boy did it hurt. Just to lay my jacket against it was painful.

But, I had found out that, **He Himself took our infirmities and bore our sicknesses** (Matt. 8:17). I had found out that, **He sent His word and healed them, and delivered them from their destructions** (Ps. 107:20). I found out that. **...by whose** (Jesus') **stripes you were healed** (1 Pet. 2:24). I found out that, "What things soever I desire when I pray to believe that I receive them, and I shall have them."(Mark 11:24 author's paraphrase.)

And so I took my Bible, stood up in my room, and called God the Father, the Holy Spirit, Jesus the Son, all the angels of heaven, all the demons of hell and Satan to record, and said, "On this day I take my stand on Mark 11:24, Matthew 8:17, Psalm 107:20 and First Peter 2:24, and I declare right now in the presence of you all, that I believe that I receive healing for this condition. I believe that this growth, whatever it is, is dead in the name of Jesus. I curse it in the name of Jesus. I command it to wither and die."

That was January of that year. January and February came, and every day for sixty days I kept saying in my prayer time, "Father, I thank You. I believe that I am healed. I received my healing for this condition the first of the year, and I believe I am healed."

Guess what? The thing got bigger and hurt worse. And every morning, when I opened my pretty brown eyes, sitting at the foot of the bed was the devil and about twelve demons. And the devil would say every day, "How do you feel?" Read this carefully. *If Satan can keep you in the realm of the senses, he will destroy you. If you keep him in the realm of faith, you will destroy him.*

So he said, "You don't look too good. How do you feel? Is it still there?" He wanted me to check it out. He wanted me to get into the natural. I said, "Devil, I did not say that I was healed because I look like it. I did not say I was healed because I felt like it. I told you sixty days ago that *I believe* I receive my healing, and I believe, right now, that I am healed." He and his little demon entourage grabbed up all their little suitcases and moved on out for that day.

Another thirty days went by. January, February and March came. The thing is growing larger. The pain is almost blinding. Terrible pain. And the devil was shooting all kinds of thoughts to my mind. "You know, people who have had the kind of growths you have, have had it turn into cancer. Now here you are. God's great man of faith and power. You are telling all these people about faith. You are telling all these people about divine healing. You are telling all these folk that God wants you well. What are they going to think when you come up dead?"

Now he is trying his fear tactics. But, I knew the Word and I knew that the Word told me, **For God has not given us a spirit of fear, but of power and of love and of a sound mind** (2 Tim. 1:7). I said, "Devil, I cannot die. If I die, God lied."

You see, I am a peculiar person in that I cannot sell something that I am not sold on. I do not care how many other people got healed. They said they got healed, I believe that. But I am the kind of person, if it is sweet, I want to taste it and know it is sweet. If it is sour I have to taste it and know that it is sour. If it works, I have to work it and know it works. That is just me. I cannot sell it to you, if I am not convinced.

I wanted this faith business to work for me. So I made my faith grow. I determined that I would not have another operation. I knew it was not a big deal to have the operation. But I did not want an operation. I wanted my faith to work. I had the Word of God. Before, when I had the operation, (there is nothing wrong with an operation), I did not know the Word. Thank God I had the first operation, it kept me alive you see, but now I had the Word and I wanted it to work.

I determined that I did not care what happened. Either one of two things was going to happen. The healing was going to manifest, or I was going to die. Either the Word works or it does not work. If it does not work, I need to find out right now. There is no point in me trying to sell something that does not work.

If I die, I will go to heaven, so there is no problem there. But that was me. That is where I was. You might think that is strange. You might think that was dumb, or stupid or even presumptuous. But wait a minute. Everything I do is in the Bible. And just because you are ignorant of the Word is not my fault.

The Kingdom Is Taken by Force

Jesus made a statement one time and said this, **And from the days of John the Baptist until now the kingdom of heaven suffers violence, and the violent take it by force** (Matt. 11:12). That is what I was doing. The reason you are taking it is not that you are taking it from God, because God is not keeping it from you, but Satan is. He will try to stop you.

He will put up roadblocks in your way to keep you from getting to the benefits of the Kingdom. That is why you have to take it by force. You are not taking it from God, but you are taking it from the devil, because he is the robber, the thief, and the murderer.

You have to take it from him, because he does not understand nice. You cannot say it "nice." You have to say, "Get back in the name of Jesus." And so I was determined that it was going to work for me. I took my stand. January, February, March, April, May and June came. Six months later the growth is bigger and the pain is worse.

Every day the devil was sitting at the foot of the bed screaming at me, "How do you feel? You don't look too good. You're going to die. It's going to turn into cancer. You are going to die and everybody's going to know you lied about healing. It did not work, Fred. If it is so good and if it works, why not for you? Why doesn't it work for you?" Every day that sucker was coming against my mind with all those thoughts.

But I said, "Devil, I do not care what you say. The Word says, 'It is forever settled in heaven' (Ps. 119:89). You are not forever settled in heaven, and the Word says, 'I am healed,' and I believe it. I believe I have received."

Every day for six months, 180 days, I kept saying, "I believe that I am healed, I believe that I am healed." To make a long story short, all the way up to November, over 300 days, I kept saying, "I believe that I am healed, I believe that I am healed, I believe that I am healed." Notice, I kept it in the present tense: "I believe I am healed." In the natural I did not feel healed. I did not look healed.

I was determined that the Word will either work for me, or it is not going to work for me. If it does not work, then I am bailing out of here. I am going on to Glory and forget about the rest of you. You get in on your own. I am going to be with the Lord, or else it is going to work.

You see, I was committed to it. That is the reason why many Christians fail to receive, because the devil backs them down, because they are not really committed. They are committed as long as it is convenient. As long as it is easy. As long as it is painless. As long as they can pop it in the microwave and pop it out, then they will go for it. But they are not going to stand for eleven months.

Sometimes that is what it takes, because that opposition that comes from Satan is designed to steal your faith. So, eleven months, three hundred and some days later, I was taking a shower as usual, and soaping up that washcloth and washing. I was washing over there on that side where that pain had been, and I did not feel the pain. I grabbed my chest, dropped the cloth, and realized that the growth was gone. Disappeared.

I do not know when it left. It had left sometime while I was asleep, because when I went to bed that night it was there. When I woke up the next day and took that shower it was gone.

Faith Must Be Developed

Now learn something. You might say, "Well, why did it take so long?" This is what you have to understand about faith. It is progressive. I was a baby in my faith development. My faith was not developed.

I had faith, but I did not know I had it, until I got into the Word and stopped asking God to give me more of it. I found out I already had it. But I had to develop it. And that is the way you develop it, by exercising it. And the way you exercise it is by confessing the Word of God over the circumstances of your life.

For eleven months or three hundred and some odd days, I had continued to say, "I believe that I am healed. I believe that I am healed." That was my faith talking. I was exercising it. And the way you exercise it is by confessing the Word of God over the circumstances of your life.

For eleven months or three hundred and some odd days, I continued to say, "I believe that I am healed. I believe that I am healed." That was my faith talking. I was exercising my faith muscle. I was pumping iron, faith wise. That is how your faith grows.

Every time I said, "I believe I am healed," my faith muscle was getting bigger. "I believe I am healed. I believe I am healed. I believe I am healed. I believe I am healed." And after about eleven months, I became Mr. Universe in my faith. I became Mr. America in my faith, glory to God. Faith drove that condition out of my body.

It does not take eleven months for those kinds of things to happen for me now, because I have been walking in it for twenty-three years. But you have to start somewhere. That is why Paul said in First Timothy 6:12, **Fight the good fight of faith.**

It is a fight because Satan is going to come against you to try to keep you from entering in. He will try to block your access into the benefits of the Kingdom. That is why you have to take it by force. You have to get violent in the Word of God and let the devil know you are not taking any mess off of him anymore. It is a warfare! It is a fight! And it is real!

I stood on the Word. He said, **And if we know that He hears us, whatever we ask, we know that we have the petitions that we have asked of Him** (1 John 5:15). We have it! How? By faith. Faith becomes our evidence of the things not seen, until such time as we actually physically see them. Do you understand this? Does this help you?

I only use healing as one illustration. But it works for anything else that you have a desire for, that is consistent with a godly life and is in line with the Word of God. But you will have to stand. As Paul said, Ephesians 6:13, **...and having done all, to stand.**

Ask Once in Faith

I said that we only ask once, but I know exactly what the devil has been saying to some of your minds. Because there are some Scriptures in the Bible, in the New Testament, that look like they contradict what I have said, or I contradict what they say. In fact, some of you may have one of those translations other than a *New King James Bible*.

I want to dispel that idea of a possible contradiction in the Scriptures, so that you are not bound up with thinking that what I am saying is unscriptural. It is very scriptural, but you have to understand what you are reading. I said, we only have to pray one time, in terms of asking or petitioning God for something. There are some Scriptures that look like what they say is to keep on asking. But you have to understand what those Scriptures are saying.

That is why the Bible says in Second Timothy 2:15: **Study to shew thyself approved unto God...** (KJV). And that is what many people do not do. They do not study. They just read in a cursory way. They pick up a little tidbit here and there, but they do not really study. So they think they are reading one thing, when in fact it may mean something else entirely.

There is a story in Luke's gospel that will illustrate what I am talking about.

Luke 11:1-4:

Now it came to pass, as He was praying in a certain place, when He ceased, that one of His disciples said to Him, "Lord, teach us to pray, as John also taught his disciples."

So He said to them, "When you pray, say: Our Father in heaven, hallowed be Your name. Your kingdom come. Your will be done on earth as it is in heaven.

"Give us day by day our daily bread. And forgive us our sins, for we also forgive everyone who is

270

indebted to us. And do not lead us into temptation, but deliver us from the evil one."

Now understand this, we do not have to pray that way because we are under the new covenant. Jesus was speaking to men under the old covenant. They were not yet in the new covenant. Why? Because the new covenant had not yet been instituted. Why? Because Jesus had not yet died and risen from the dead. Until He died and rose from the dead, you could not have a new covenant. If you do not have a new one you still had to be operating under the old one.

He gave them this, what tradition has called, *The Lord's Prayer*. He gave them that formula, to finish out the old covenant. What has happened, sad to say, is that we have drug that same modus operandi into the new covenant and tried to make it work. We do not have to pray that way.

He told them to pray that way, because they were on the other side of the new covenant. They had to pray that way, because they did not have the right to pray like we do, because they were not yet born again. They were not new creatures in Christ Jesus, so they did not have the rights that we have. They did not have the covenant that we have.

Luke 11:5-13:

And He said to them, "Which of you shall have a friend, and go to him at midnight and say to him, 'Friend, lend me three loaves; for a friend of mine has come to me on his journey, and I have nothing to set before him'; and he will answer from within and say, 'Do not trouble me; the door is now shut, and my children are with me in bed; I cannot rise and give to you'?

"I say to you, though he will not rise and give to him because he is his friend, yet because of his persistence he will rise and give him as many as he needs.

"So I say to you, ask, and it will be given to you; seek, and you will find; knock, and it will be opened to

271

you. For everyone who asks receives and he who seeks finds; and to him who knocks it will be opened.

"If a son ask for bread from any father among you, will he give him a stone? Or if he asks for a fish, will he give him a serpent instead of a fish? Or if he asks for an egg, will he offer him a scorpion?

"If you then, being evil, know how to give good gifts to your children, how much more will your heavenly Father give the Holy Spirit to those who ask Him!"

You Only Have To Ask Once for the Holy Spirit

We had to read all those verses in sequential order to get the import of this story. Now let me ask you a question. How many times, biblically speaking, do you believe that a person has to ask God to give them the Holy Spirit? One time? Right! If you only have to ask once to get the Holy Spirit, why would you have to ask five times to get your healing, seven times to get a new house, three times for a new job, fourteen times for a new car? That would be somewhat confusing, because I would not know how many times to apply to each event in life.

If I only have to ask one time for the Holy Spirit, then I only have to ask one time for the healing. I mean that seems logical, does it not? Go back to verse 9. He said, **So I say to you, ask, and it will be given to you....**

There are other translations, but sometimes they can be misleading. For instance, the *Amplified Bible*. Verse 9, reads: **So I say to you, Ask and keep on asking and it shall be given you; seek and keep on seeking and you shall find; knock and keep on knocking and the door shall be opened to you.** *The Living Bible* says it this way: **And so it is with prayer—keep on asking and you will keep on getting....** Now here is what happens. When you read that in the *Amplified* and *Living* Bibles, you get the impression from the context, from the story of the man knocking on the door for the bread, that you "ask and keep on asking," because that is what the man in the story did. He kept on asking, and he finally got it. So people say, "That is what I will do. I will keep on asking God, and I will finally get healed."

But friend, just think about what we have already covered. That would violate First John 5:15 and Mark 11:24. **And if we know that He hears us, whatever we ask, we know that we have the petitions that we have asked of Him."** Jesus said **"...What things soever ye desire, when ye pray, believe that ye receive them, and ye shall have them.**

He did not say, "What things soever you desire when you pray keep on asking, and you will finally get them." So now we have a dilemma, because this verse in Luke 11, verse 9 tied in with that story of the man continuing to ask for the bread, sounds very plausible. "Well, that is what you do. You just keep asking God till you get it." But that would not be faith.

What Is the Story Really Saying?

What we have to do is go back and examine the story and find out what the story is *really* saying. Is the story really telling us that is how the man got the bread, because he kept right on asking? No! Let us now go back in the story to verse 8. Look at the word *persistence* (in the *King James Version* the word is *importunity*), and that is where the people who translated this no doubt got this idea of saying, "Ask and keep asking." They are not understanding the spirit of what is being declared.

The story looks like the man got what he wanted, simply because he kept on persisting in asking. That is a part of what the word *importunity* means. It means to ask. It means to keep on asking. It means to continue to do so. But there is another facet to that word. There is another aspect of the meaning, that no one ever deals with. Not only does it mean to ask and keep on asking, but it also means to ask without shame.

It means to ask on the basis of the fact that you have a *right* to ask whoever it is you are asking, and you have a *right* to expect to receive what you are asking for. Not just keep on asking, but the fact that as you ask, you have a right to do it. You are doing it without any sense of shame.

Let us look at the story more closely. Verse 5, **And He said to them, "Which of you shall have a friend, and go to him at midnight."** Underline the word *friend*. It did not say employee or employer. It did not say relative. In other words, there was not anything legally here in reference to an employer-employee relationship. Neither was there anything by blood, in terms of a relationship. He said, a friend. **Which of you shall have a friend, and go to him at midnight....**

Right away that ought to tell you something. That is a strange time to come to someone's house and expect to get some bread. **And go to him at midnight and say to him, "Friend, lend me three loaves...."** Now right here ought to alert you to something else. He said, "Lend me." When we pray, we are not asking God to lend us anything. I am asking to be healed. Not to lend me some healing. He says, **Lend me three loaves.** Verse 6, **For a friend of mine has come to me on his journey, and I have nothing to set before him.** Verse 7, **And he will answer from within and say, "Do not trouble me."**

In other words he is saying, "Man, don't bug me now. The door is shut. The cat is out, the dog is in. The children are with me in bed. My wife is right beside me, warm and comfy. I can't get up and give you any bread right now. And besides that, what are you doing out here at midnight anyway?"

Then his wife is chiming in and says, "Who is that?" "It's John. He needs some bread." She says, "Tell that fool to go home. Doesn't he have any better sense messing with us here at twelve o'clock at night? What's wrong with him?" Follow on now—verse 6: **"For a friend of mine has come to me on his journey, and I have nothing to set before him." And he will answer from within and say, "Do not trouble me; the door is now shut, and my children are with me in bed; I cannot rise and give to you." I say to you, though he will not rise and give to him because he is his friend, yet because of his persistence....**

The Man Did Not Keep Asking

Now notice this, that in the story, it *does not* tell us that the man kept on asking. He only asked one time as far as the story was told. But Jesus used the word *persistence*, because that word carries the idea that the man on the outside was saying, in essence, "That's my friend on the inside. I have a right because of our friendship to be here at midnight to ask him for some bread."

Folks are passing up and down the street. Police cars are driving up and down the street and this fool is out here at midnight, knocking on someone's door. He might get arrested for disturbing the peace. But he was unashamed to knock on that door, because, "That is my friend inside, and I am his friend, and I have a right to expect my friend to respond to our friendship."

That is what the story is about. Not about *keep on asking*. Because if you notice the story very carefully, the man only asked one time. As I told you before, he did not keep on asking.

Jesus Never Said To Keep on Asking

Jesus never said, "Keep on asking." Jesus said, **I say to you, though he will not rise and give to him because he** is his friend, yet because of his persistence he will rise and give him as many as he needs. "So I say to you, ask and it will be given to you; seek, and you will find; knock, and it will be opened to you."

But only knock once. He is not telling you to knock more than once. Just one time. Now, follow the rest of the story. He said, verse 10, **For everyone who asks receives.** He did not say, "Everyone who keeps on asking." He said, **...everyone who asks receives....**

Wait a minute! I thought we just read it. **And if we know that He hears us, whatever we ask, we know that *we have* the petitions...** (1 John 5:15).

If I have it by faith, I cannot ask for it again. So it is an erroneous translation to say, "Ask and keep on asking," *unless the implication is never give up the asking process.* But not necessarily saying, ask for the same thing over and over, because that would be a violation of faith. Can you see that? Verse 10 again, **For everyone who asks receives....**

If You Do Not Receive, You Didn't Ask

I am frank to tell you that if you did not receive what you asked for, you did not ask. You thought you did, but you did not ask. I said you thought you did, but you did not ask. Because if you asked and you did not receive, then Jesus lied to you. Then we would need to close the church down and get rid of all the Bibles, because Jesus would be a liar.

Jesus would have to be a liar if you say you asked and you did not receive, because He said, **...Ask, and it will be given to you.** He did not say, "Ask and there is a 60/40 chance that you might get it if it is leap year, and all the stars are in proper conjunction, and all the planets are in their proper place, it just might work." He did not say that, did He? He said, **Ask, and it will be given to you.**

24

The Right and Wrong Way To Ask

There is a right and a wrong way to ask. You can be ever so sincere, but be sincerely wrong. Now I have used this illustration before, but I think it is a classic, and it illustrates what we are talking about. Because the Bible says in John 14:6, that Jesus is the way, the truth and the life.

It does not say that "Jesus is the way, the *lie* and the life." It says He is the truth. That means He deals in truth, which means He tells the truth. So if He said, **Ask, and it will be given to you,** and you ask and it is not given to you, then the fault has to lie with the asker. Otherwise Jesus lied. If He lied about that, He may have lied about other things and we are in trouble anyway. Right? So if you did not get it, then you did not ask, not according to biblical asking principles.

Sincerity Doesn't Get Prayers Answered

I will illustrate this by a personal experience that I had, to show you that you can be ever so sincere and in need and yet your prayer or your request can go unanswered if you are not asking correctly.

I was in grammar school and the teacher had given us an assignment in the classroom. She gave out paper, pencils, and instructions. We were supposed to do a certain project in the classroom. The teacher said, "Upon completion of the project, if by chance any student completed the project before the end of the class session, you may be permitted to leave the class early and go on to the play yard and play ahead of the recess bell ringing."

As time went on, the clock was ticking away, and one by one different students finished, and left the room. Finally, I finished before the bell rang. I went up to the desk, where the teacher was seated reading. I put my pencil in the little box. I put my paper on the stack with the other papers as I was instructed to do, and then I said to the teacher, "Can I go outside and play now?"

The teacher looked up from her book and said, "Can you?" Again I said, "Can I go outside and play? I have finished my assignment ahead of schedule, and you said that if we finished we could go outside and play. So what I want to know is, can I go outside and play now?"

The teacher said, "Can you?" I am getting a little frustrated at this point, because I do not understand what is going on. I was just a little kid, in the process of learning. And so I said it the third time, "Please, can I go outside and play?" And the teacher looked at me and said, "Can you?" I said it for the fourth time, "Can I go outside and play?" The teacher said, "Can you?"

I am totally demoralized at this point and she could see that I was. She took the opportunity to teach me a very important lesson in English. I learned the lesson so well that I have never forgotten it over all of these years. You see, when I said, "Can I go outside and play," what I was actually saying was, do I have the ability to go outside and play? And so the teacher was saying "Can you?" In other words, do you have the ability?

Permission Versus Ability

But that is not what I needed at that time. At that time I did not need to know, *can I*, I needed to know, *may I*. I needed *permission*, not *ability*, to do it, yet both of them are asking. But in that context it was the wrong asking.

What I needed to know was, *may I.* May I is permission to. Can I is, *do I have the ability to?* I was sincere, but I was sincerely wrong. And that is the way we can be with God. We can be sincere and in desperate need, in pain while we are asking, and it never comes to pass, because we are asking *can we,* when we should say, *may we.* Do you see the difference? Jesus said to ask, and it will be given to you. So if you did not get, you did not ask. Maybe you have been saying, "can I," when you should have been saying, "may I." Do you understand what I mean?

Maybe you did not use the right rule. He goes on to say, **Ask, and it will be given to you; seek, and you will find; knock, and it will be opened to you. For everyone who asks receives, and he who seeks finds, and to him who knocks it will be opened. If a son....**

Here is another aspect of this story that I want to emphasize. He said, **If a son asks for bread from any father among you, will he give him a stone?** (Of course not!) **Or if he asks for a fish, will he give him a serpent** (a snake) **instead of a fish?** (No parent in their right mind would.) **Or if he asks for an egg, will he offer him a scorpion?** (Of course not!) He goes on to say, **If you then, being evil, know how to give good gifts to your children, how much more will your heavenly Father give the Holy Spirit to those who ask Him!**

God Does Not Deny Our Desires

Here is the issue that I really want to get to. I can remember forty years ago when I first got saved, joined the church, started going to church, and started trying to pray. I would ask for something, (I did not know what I was doing, and did not know that I did not know what I was doing), and get something else, or something else would come.

Then my dear precious brethren in the church would say, "Dear Brother Price, you prayed for a Cadillac and you got a Volkswagen. But God knew that it would be better for you to have the Volkswagen, because if you got that Cadillac you might not want to come to church anymore. You might be tempted to turn away from God. So God, in order to keep you humble, knew it was best for you to have the Volkswagen. So just accept it and know that God knows best."

Have you ever heard anything similar to that? Sure you have. That is why I want to point this out, because that is unscriptural. In fact, if you asked for a Cadillac and got a Volkswagen, I am frank to tell you, God did not answer your prayer. Now how do I know that. Right here, verse 11: **If a son asks for bread from any father among you, will he give him a stone?**

We could read it like this, "If a son of God shall ask God for a Cadillac, will He give him a Volkswagen?" No! Absolutely not. **If you then, being evil, know how to give good gifts to your children, how much more will your heavenly Father give the Holy Spirit to those who ask Him.**

If you only have to ask one time for the Holy Spirit, you only have to ask one time for anything else. But of course you have to ask in faith. So if you pray for a dog and you get a cat, God did not answer your prayer. Your prayer did not get answered. So at that time I accepted that, because I thought these people knew what they were talking about. And it seemed like that was reasonable.

But you know that is so stupid, because if that were true, that God is going to give us what He wants us to have, why should we even waste time praying? Why not just give us what He knows we ought to have to keep us humble?

No, I am telling you if you asked for a red tie and got a green one, God did not answer that prayer. Now I will tell you what God will do. If you ask for a red tie and end up with both a green and red tie, that is God. Because He always gives good measure, pressed down, shaken together and running over. You may get more but you will never get less.

What is this story about the man asking for bread at midnight telling us? If it is not telling us to keep asking for the same thing, what is it telling us?

What this story is all about is a contrast. Here was a man who went to another man who was no more to him than a friend. No blood ties. No family ties. Not an employer, employee, where there might have been some legal ramifications. Just a friend. He went at midnight, and asked for bread and got what he wanted, because he asked without shame, of someone who was no more to him than a friend.

He had no right to demand it and say, "You have to give it to me, because you are my cousin. You have to give it to me, because I am your employer." No, just a friend. Now here is the contrast. Jesus is saying, "If that man could get what he wanted from someone who was no more to him than a friend, how much more can you, blood-bought, blood-washed, filled with the Spirit, with a better covenant established upon better promises, get what you need?"

God Told You To Ask, Seek and Knock

Jesus is the One Who told you to come, and to seek, and to knock and to ask. Surely you can expect to receive exactly what you asked for, because you have a covenant right to it. Glory to God! It is a contrast. This man got it because he was unashamed to ask of a friend. I have a heavenly Father Who has bought and paid for me, and who has given me a *commandment* to come to Him and ask. We have a right to it!

Some Christians get real scary when you start talking about rights. They say, "We do not have any rights, Brother Price. That is audacious of you to say such a thing. We must always say the will of the Lord be done. We must always say, if it be Thy will."

No! That is not Bible. That is Sunday school literature. That is denominationalism. That is theology. But that is not *Bible*. He said it. We read it, **...What things soever ye desire, when ye pray, believe that ye receive them...** (KJV). Not something like them. Not something that looks like them. Not something that God thinks is better for you. **...What things soever ye desire, when ye pray, believe that ye receive them** (them desires), **and ye shall have them** (KJV).

If I ask in line with the Word of God, I have a right to expect to be heard, because He is the One Who told me to come. In verse 9, He said (and this is the main man speaking. This is, "El Capitán," speaking. This is "El Presidente," speaking. This is the "Man!" "Christ!" "Messiah!" "Savior!") **So I say to you, ask, and it will be given to you....** Now what else do you need? Do you want Him to send you an RSVP? The Man said, "Ask!" We do not have a right because we have a right, we have a right because He has given us that option to come to Him.

It is not like we are doing something against God. He is the One Who invited us to come. He is the One Who said, **Ask, and you will receive** (John 16:24). He is the One Who said, **What things soever ye desire, when ye pray, believe that ye receive them, and ye shall have them** (KJV). He is the One who said, **Now this is the confidence that we have in Him, that if we ask anything according to His will, He hears us.**

So we have a right, because we are blood-bought and blood-washed. We are children of the King. We have a covenant, a contract that guarantees it to us. We have a right to come. But, we have to come in line with the program. We have to come in line with the rules, the regulations and the laws that govern and control it, and when we do, it will work for us, over and over and over again.

There is no maybe. It will work, absolutely, positively. But you have to work it in line with the Word. So if you keep on asking, "Lord, give it to me, Lord, give it to me," the same thing over and over and over again, it is not going to work. You are going to nullify your prayer.

You only pray one time when it comes to a petition prayer. Understand that! We are not teaching on the subject of prayer, and there are other kinds of prayer. But when it comes to petition prayer or the prayer of faith, if you ask more than once you are saying by your asking that you did not believe that you received it the first time.

Let us look at another roadblock. In Luke 18 there is another story that people have used as a reason for praying over and over for the same thing.

Luke 18:1-8:

> Then He spoke a parable to them, that men always ought to pray and not lose heart, saying: "There was in a certain city a judge who did not fear God nor regard man. Now there was a widow in that city; and she came to him, saying, 'Get justice for me from my adversary.'
>
> "And he would not for a while; but afterward he said within himself, 'Though I do not fear God nor regard man, yet because this widow troubles me I will avenge her, lest by her continual coming she weary me.'"
>
> Then the Lord said, "Hear what the unjust judge said. And shall God not avenge His own elect who cry out day and night to Him, though He bear long with them? I tell you that He will avenge them speedily. Nevertheless, when the Son of Man comes, will He really find faith on the earth?"

A parable is a spiritual truth or law set in the context of a natural situation. In other words, a natural illustration to point up a spiritual truth. **Then He spoke a parable to them, that men always ought to pray and not lose heart.**

Always ought to pray means that we should never give up prayer as a means of communication with the Father. *Lose heart* means to get weak, discouraged, throw up your hands and give it up as a lost cause. You could be tempted to do that if you pray five hundred times and never get any answers. I did that, because I never got any answers. I said, "There is no point in this, I am wasting my time."

My church, unfortunately, did not tell me that I was not doing it right, because they did not know themselves. And Jesus did say words to the effect, "When the blind lead the blind, they both end up in the microwave oven."

That is where I was, in the microwave. Do you know what I mean? I never got any answers so I got tired of doing it. I got tired of praying. I said, "What is the point in this? This is a waste of time!" So I went for years and never really prayed because I did not know what I was doing. I figured, "If God wants me to have it, He will give it to me," but He won't. That will not work either.

Notice that there is a question mark after the word earth, which looks like He is asking a question. I submit that He is not asking a question. He knows what He will find when He comes back. He actually made a statement designed to arrest our attention. Let me ask you a question, and I will show you what I am talking about. How many of you know that one of the attributes of God is called "omnipresence"? That simply means that God is present everywhere at the same time.

If we were to go back to the book of Genesis, we would find where it talks about Adam and Eve in the garden. It says that the Lord God came walking in the garden in the cool of the day and God said "Adam, where are you?" with a question mark. (Gen. 3:8,9.)

How could God ask a question like that, if God is omnipresent? God would have known where Adam was. So in reality it was not a question. It was a statement designed to arrest Adam's attention to let him know the gravity of the situation that he had jumped into by his act of rebellion.

...Nevertheless, when the Son of Man comes, will He really find faith on the earth? He knows exactly what He is going to find. He is saying that, because it takes faith to pray. He is talking about prayer. It said that He spoke the parable, **...that men always ought to pray and not lose heart**. I say it again, it takes faith to pray. So He said, "Will He really find faith when He comes back?" to arrest our attention to the fact that it takes faith to pray.

He knows He will find faith on the earth, because people are going to be praying. When He comes back there will be Christians on the earth, because that is why He is coming back, to receive the Christians. So if they are here, they will be praying.

Now let us go back and look at the story in detail. What is the purpose of this story? It is identical with the purpose of chapter 11. It is showing a contrast. Now watch it. Here is a woman, not even married, but a widow. She comes to a judge, who did not fear God, or regard man.

Here comes this widow to this judge, and she got what she wanted. Not because the judge feared God, not even because the judge wanted to answer her request. But the judge said, "If I don't do something, this old lady is going to drive me crazy. The easiest way to get rid of her is to answer her request and she is out of here and I am free of her."

You Have a Better Covenant

What this story is showing us is a contrast. Here is a widow who came to a judge who did not fear God or regard man and got exactly what she wanted only because of the potential of continuing to come and finally wearing the judge out. So he capitulated and gave in to her, simply to get rid of her.

What Jesus is saying to us is, "You are a blood- bought, blood-washed, born-again, Spirit-filled believer. You have a better covenant established upon better promises. If this lady could get what she wanted for no more than the potential of wearing out this judge, how much more can you expect to get what you want when you come to the judge of all the ages?" That is the gist of the story.

There are those who have taught that this story represents the Christian and God. Have you ever heard that? That could not possibly be true, because that would make God a no-caring Judge, which He is not. And it would make His reason for answering your request, to get rid of you. And that is not why God answers prayer. If God did not want to be bothered with you, He would not have said, "Ask!" Are you following me? So God wants to be "bothered" with you. It is not a bother.

Jesus told this story to show us a contrast. God is not going to answer your request just to get rid of you. In fact, if you do not come correctly, in line with His Word, He does not hear you anyway. It does not register. It does not compute. Now let me ask you a question. It would be a lot easier to know something, or see something, or understand something when it manifests itself right in front of you, right? That would be easier than having to pray and believe that you receive something that you cannot see, and having to wait for it to be manifested in the course of time.

It seems like it would be a lot easier just to pop it up here in front of me. Then I would know it! I would not have to believe it! I could contact it with my senses. Now why is it that God requires me, when I pray, to believe that I have received my desire? Why put me through these changes of having to believe that I receive the very moment that I pray, when I could simply wait for it to come, for God to give it to me, and then I would know that I had it?

That is a good question. There is a reason for this, and you need to understand the reason. We will now look at the reason.

God Does Not Operate in Time

2 Peter 3:8:

> **But, beloved, do not forget this one thing, that with the Lord one day is as a thousand years, and a thousand years as one day.**

Many say the way that you interpret time prophetically with God is that one day equals one thousand years. This verse, among others, has been used to prove that point. Because it says right here, **...with the Lord one day is as a thousand years, and a thousand years as one day**.

But I would like to suggest to you that this is not what this verse is talking about at all. I believe that this verse is talking about a truth that is far deeper than trying to figure out one day equals a thousand years. Now let me suggest this: **But, beloved, do not forget this one thing, that with the Lord one day is as....** Right after the word *is*, it says *as*. In your Bible, draw a circle around the word *as*. Make a line from that circle to any empty space close by in which you can insert the work *like*.

That is the way we talk. "You know, *like* a so-and-so." Here is the way that would read. "But, beloved, do not forget this one thing, that with the Lord one day is *like* a thousand years." Understand, He is not saying *it is* a thousand years, He is saying that to God, that is what it is like.

In other words, to God, one day is just like a thousand years. Or He could have said, two thousand years, five thousand years, ten thousand years, twenty thousand years, fifty thousand years, one hundred thousand years. Why? Because God has no yesterdays, and God has no tomorrows. There are no clocks in heaven, nor are there any calendars. And God never, ever has a birthday. The only reason *you* have a birthday is because you are recognizing your point of origin, because you know you have a point of ending.

God has no beginning, and God has no ending. So He does not need any clocks, because time is irrelevant to God. He is not bound by time. He is no older today than He was yesterday, than He will be tomorrow. In fact, look at this very carefully. Here is a divine law for you. *God lives in one eternal now*. There is no yesterday with God, and there is no tomorrow with God. He lives in one eternal now.

Let me illustrate. Picture if you would, an athletic field in the middle of a stadium, with a standard running track around the field. Those tracks are usually a quarter mile around or 440 yards. Think of that track, one quarter mile around, as eternity in which God lives.

Take a strand of hair, representing 10,000 years of time, and place it on the track. Then take a strand of hair, one by one, and lay it side by side all the way around the track. Remember each strand of hair equals 10,000 years of what we call time. That would represent a lot of time to us, but to God it would be like a day, or like *now* or *present tense*.

God lives in one eternal now. All of this ties in with why God says, "When you pray, believe you receive." The reason that you have to believe, when you pray, that you receive your heart's desire, is that if you do not believe that you receive it when you pray, God has no other time to hear you. God cannot hear or answer it tomorrow, because He does not have a tomorrow in which to answer it. He only has now, or today, and if you do not believe you receive now, God cannot do anything about it later, because He has no tomorrow.

PART VII

FIGHT THE GOOD
FIGHT OF FAITH

25
God Is a NOW God

God is a present tense God. Do you understand that? Jesus said that when you pray you should believe that you receive. When? When you pray. Why? Because when you pray is *now*. And that is when God hears. God cannot hear you tomorrow. *We* have a tomorrow, but God does not. God only has now.

Let me show you a little more graphically what I am talking about. In Exodus 3, we have the story of Moses out in the field watching over his father-in-law Jethro's sheep. Moses looked up one day and saw a bright, shiny light on a hillside. It looked like fire, but he did not know exactly what it was. He came to it, and he saw a bush, or foliage, and it appeared to be on fire, but it was not consumed.

He said, "Let me turn aside and see this great sight." So he came near to it, and God spoke to him.

Exodus 3:7-10:
And the Lord said: "I have surely seen the oppression of My people who are in Egypt, and have heard their cry because of their taskmasters, for I know their sorrows.

"So I have come down to deliver them out of the hand of the Egyptians, and to bring them up from that land to a good and large land, to a land flowing with milk and honey, to the place of the Canaanites and the Hittites and the Amorites and the Perizzites and the Hivites and the Jebusites.

"Now therefore, behold, the cry of the children of Israel has come to Me, and I have also seen the oppression with which the Egyptians oppress them. Come now, therefore, and I will send you to Pharaoh that you may bring My people, the children of Israel, out of Egypt."

Now Moses began to remonstrate with God. He said, "Now wait a minute, Lord. Whoa, You know they just kicked me out of there about forty years ago, and they revoked my driver's license, and my social security card is invalid at this time." He began to see the enormity of God sending him back and he tried to get out of it. He said, "Now, Lord, You know I do not speak too well, I stutter. How am I going to speak to Pharaoh?"

God told Moses He would send Aaron to be his mouthpiece, so he could not use that as an alibi. Finally, Moses said to God, "Now wait a minute, Lord. If I go down there and tell Pharaoh to let the people go, he may lock me up and throw away the key. And besides that, who am I going to say sent me?"

I want you to look at this closely, because this is very important. Verses 13,14:

> Then Moses said to God, "Indeed, when I come to the children of Israel and say to them, 'The God of your fathers has sent me to you,' and they say to me, 'What is His name?' what shall I say to them?"

> And God said to Moses, "I AM WHO I AM." And He said, "Thus you shall say to the children of Israel, 'I AM has sent me to you.'"

God Is Always Present Tense

What a name. *I AM.* Now, Jesus said, **...when you pray, believe that you receive....** We found out "now faith is." Not tomorrow faith will be, not yesterday faith was, but now faith is. *Now* is present tense. God did not say to Moses, "You go tell the children of Israel that I *was* has sent you. Do not tell them that I *will be* someday has sent you.

You tell them, that I AM has sent you." *I AM is present tense,* which means *now.*

What a name! If you do not get the revelation from that, you never will. He did not say, "Tell them that Jehovah has sent you." And yet that was His name. "Do not tell them that Almighty God, the Creator of the heavens and the earth, has sent you." And yet that is Who He is. "Just tell them that I AM who I AM has sent you." He did not say, "I am that I was," or "I am that I will be." He said, "I AM Who I AM." I say it again, "I AM" is present tense. Right now! *When* you pray, you have to believe that you receive. And is it not interesting that the Son of God, born as it were in God's own household, Messiah, Jesus, Who was with the Father God in eternity past, when He came to the world picked up on His Father's modus operandi, and every time He referred to Himself, He said, "*I AM!*"

Revelation 1:18:

I am He who lives, and was dead, and behold, I am alive forevermore. Amen. And I have the keys of Hades and of Death....

Revelation 1:11:

...I am the Alpha and the Omega, the First and the Last....

John 10:7:

I am the door of the sheep.

John 10:11:

I am the good shepherd....

John 14:6:

...I am the way....

I AM. That is present tense. He could have said, "I was, I used to be or someday I will be." No! He said, "I AM." That is present tense. That is why you have to believe you receive it now, because God is I AM. God is not *going to be,* God is not *used to be.* He is I AM, and "I AM" is present tense.

Now look at Hebrews 13:8: **Jesus Christ is the same yesterday, today, and forever.** Isn't that the same thing as saying, "I AM?" Everything that He was yesterday He is today. Everything that He is today He was yesterday. Everything that He was yesterday He will be tomorrow. And everything that He will be tomorrow He will be forever. Why? Because He is the same yesterday, today and forever.

That is the same as saying, "I AM." Now why should you be continuously saying, "I believe that I have received?" Because you are making a confession of faith. Why should you continuously make that confession of faith? Because you have a malevolent spiritual adversary, Satan by name, who wants to keep you from entering into the fullness of the things of God. He has angels and demons who will try to hinder you or stop your answer from coming through from the spirit world.

Your continuous, unwavering confession of faith throws the battle to you. Some stop standing because it is taking too long. God is too slow. It did not come when we thought it should. So the demonic forces come in and steal your blessings and keep them from coming.

Now let me give you a Bible illustration that will blow your mind concerning this principle. Just before showing you this illustration, let me remind you of the words of Jesus in Mark 11:23, **For assuredly, I say to you, whoever says to this mountain, 'Be removed and be cast into the sea,' and does not doubt in his heart, but believes that those things he says will be done, he will have whatever he says.** If he does not doubt in his heart. Jesus said in Mark 11:24, **...When you pray....**

26
Having Done All, Stand

You cannot pray without saying. So they are tied together. Actually that is all that prayer is—saying something. You are not thinking something, you are saying something. "Lord, I believe I receive. Thank You, Father."

I have to continue to say that, because as I said before, there is a spiritual war going on out there. Satan does not want your desire to come to pass in your life and so you have to stand for the things that you are believing God for.

You have to stand against the opposition that Satan will bring against you. It will manifest through the circumstances. But it is spiritual influences that are behind that, to try to keep those things from coming to you.

Here is the perfect illustration that I spoke of earlier.

Daniel 10:10,11:

Suddenly, a hand touched me, which made me tremble on my knees and on the palms of my hands. And he said to me, "O Daniel, man greatly beloved, understand the words that I speak to you, and stand upright, for I have now been sent to you." While he was speaking this word to me, I stood trembling.

Here is the story. Daniel had a vision. He did not understand the vision completely and he prayed and asked God for the understanding of it. It was a while before that understanding came to him. This is comparable to us when we believe we receive, and make our confession of faith.

I told you there can be a time span between the time that you claim something by faith until you physically see it. It might be because of the thing that you are believing God for, which might be bigger than your faith can handle right now. It may take a little longer for your faith to produce it.

Remember, I told you, it is really not God Who answers the prayer, *and yet it is God* in the sense that God has made the provisions. Because everything needed to answer all your prayers is already here in the earth realm. You have never had a prayer answered where something dropped out of heaven and came down into your bedroom or living room or car or wherever you were. Whatever that answer was, it came from this earth realm, did it not?

Daniel Had To Fight Through Prayer

That is the background of the story. Daniel had a vision. He did not completely understand the vision so he prayed about it. Now watch this—verse 11, again:

> And he said to me, "O Daniel, man greatly beloved, understand the words that I speak to you, and stand upright, for I have now been sent to you." While he was speaking this word to me, I stood trembling.

Watch this now.

> Then he said to me, "Do not fear, Daniel, for from the first day that you set your heart to understand, and to humble yourself before your God, *your words were heard*; and I have come *because of your words*"(v.12).

The angel came because of his words. Our words have power with God. Our words have life in them. The angel in essence, said, "I did not come for you, I came for your words." He said, "Your prayer was heard the very first day." He said, "I have come because of your words."

Verse 13:

> "But the prince of the kingdom of Persia withstood me twenty-one days; and behold, Michael, one of the

**chief princes, came to help me, for I had been left alone
there with the kings of Persia."**

Now this king of Persia, or prince of Persia, is not
talking about a physical flesh and blood monarch sitting on
a throne. It is talking about the demon spirit that had been
assigned to Persia. And the name of that spirit was the
prince of Persia.

This angel said that the prince of the kingdom of Persia
withstood him. Even in the spirit world there is warfare
going on. The angels are in conflict. The angels of Satan
against the angels of God. Listen to him. He said, **But the
prince of the kingdom of Persia withstood me twenty-one
days; and behold, Michael....**

Michael was an angel. The angel was saying in essence,
"Daniel, because of your persistence in not giving up on
your request, because you continued to keep your word on
that which your heart desired, I have come for your words.
He said, **but the prince of the kingdom of Persia withstood
me twenty-one days....**

For three weeks this warfare was going on in the spirit
world. That is why sometimes it takes three weeks for your
answer to come. It is not because God *has not* dispatched the
answer. The angel said to Daniel, "You were heard that very
first day you prayed. The first time you opened your mouth
God heard it and the answer was on its way, but the prince
of Persia is out there fighting against you."

That is why you have to continue to make your
confession of faith. When you make your confession of
faith, you throw the battle to the angels of God, so that they
can overcome the angels of Satan, and get here with your
answer. Back to verse 12 again. **Then said he unto me, Fear
not, Daniel: for from the first day...** (KJV). *What first day?*
The only day God could hear him. The *now*. The *I AM. The
present tense.*

God Only Hears in the Present

That is why when you pray you have to believe you receive it—it is the only time God can hear it. And because of the warfare going on in the spirit world, you have to continue to say, "I believe that I have received. I believe that I have received. I believe my need is met. I believe I have it now."

When you do that, you are throwing the battle to the angels of God who are fighting against the angels of Satan. There is warfare going on out there in the spirit realm, and those angels of God can only get through based upon your confession of faith. When you back off and you give up, you throw the battle to the angels of Satan and they have a right to hinder that thing and keep it from coming.

God heard your prayer the very first day. That is why you have to have confidence to know, "I prayed and God heard me. My answer is on its way. Thank You, Father. I believe I have received." And I do not care what happens, hell or high water, low water or no water, polluted water, blue water, green water, murky water, whatever kind of water, you have to stand. And having done all, to stand.

You Must Be Willing To Stand Forever

You have to be willing to make a commitment and stand, if it takes twenty-seven million years. That is the kind of attitude that you have to have. Otherwise, Satan will back you down. That is why many Christians never succeed, because they go so far, as long as it is easy. They go so far as long as there is no opposition. As long as no one resists them they will stand. Everything you want is already in the spirit world. Your faith is what brings it into visibility.

When I was in high school I took a course in photography. At that time they did not have the Polaroid cameras and all the instant photography that they have now. We had to do our own developing.

I was in this particular photography class, and the teacher was teaching us some principles about photography. We were in this room and it was dark. I did not understand at first why the room was dark. There was a red light on and we could barely see. On the table the professor had placed three pans of crystal clear water—I thought.

Then the professor took a sheet of white paper with nothing on it—I thought. He took the paper and put it in the first pan of water and began to slosh it around. I could not understand why in the world he was doing that. The paper seemed clean to me. It did not seem as though the paper needed a bath. Why was he putting it in the water? I thought it was water. But in reality it was not.

Then as I watched that paper sloshing around in that pan, slowly but surely an image began to appear on that paper. It got clearer, and clearer, and clearer, and clearer. Finally, there was a photograph of someone that came off of that plain piece of paper that did not have anything on it originally—I thought. Then he took it out of the first pan of crystal clear water—I thought, and put it in the second pan of crystal clear water—I thought. He sloshed it around a little more, put it in the third pan of crystal clear water, which was actually water, washed that photograph off, took a clothes pin, and hung that picture on a line.

Here is my point. The first pan of water had a developing solution in it. The second pan of water had a fixing solution in it. And the third pan of water was to wash off the first two chemicals. When he put it in the water which was actually a developing solution or chemical, it was not the chemical that put the portrait on the paper. The image was already there (on the paper) in the spirit world, but it took the developing solution to bring it out into visibility.

It takes your faith to bring it out of the spirit world. It is out there. The picture is there. Your house is there. Your car is there. Your wife is there. Your husband is there. Your baby is there. Your business is there. Your degree is there. Your money is there. *Whatever* you need is there. Use your faith and bring it in. It is there. Use your faith and develop your picture. Do not doubt it. It is right there, on the pages of the Word of God. Submit it to the solution, the developer, and that is your faith. Hallelujah!

Frederick K. C. Price, Ph.D., founded Crenshaw Christian Center in Los Angeles, California, in 1973, with a congregation of about 300 people. Today, the church numbers well over 16,000 people of various racial backgrounds.

Crenshaw Christian Center, home of the renowned 10,146 seat FaithDome, has a staff of more than 250 employees. Included on its thirty acre grounds are a Ministry Training Institute, the Crenshaw Christian Center Correspondence School, the Frederick K.C. Price III elementary and junior and senior high schools, as well as the FKCP III Child Care Center.

The *Ever Increasing Faith* television and radio broadcasts are outreaches of Crenshaw Christian Center. The television program is viewed on over 100 stations throughout the United States and overseas. The radio program airs on over forty stations across the country.

Dr. Price travels extensively, teaching on the Word of Faith forcefully, in the power of the Holy Spirit. He is the author of over thirty books on the subjects of faith and divine healing.

In 1990, Dr. Price founded the Fellowship of Inner City Word of Faith Ministries (FICWFM) for the purpose of fostering and spreading the faith message among independent ministries located in urban, metropolitan areas of the United States.

Other Books by Fred Price

Faith's Greatest Enemies

Name It and Claim It
The Power of Positive Confession

Practical Suggestions
for Successful Ministry

Prosperity on God's Terms

Concerning Them
Which Are Asleep

Marriage and the Family
Practical Insight for Family Living

High Finance
God's Financial Plan
Tithes and Offerings
Living in the Realm of the Spirit

Is Healing for All?

How To Obtain Strong Faith
Six Principles

The Holy Spirit—The Missing Ingredient

Faith, Foolishness or Presumption?

Thank God for Everything?

The Origin of Satan

Now Faith Is

The Faithfulness of God

The Promised Land

The Victorious, Overcoming Life

How To Believe God for a Mate

Available from your local bookstore.

Harrison House
Tulsa, Oklahoma 74153

For a complete list of tapes and books by Fred Price,
or to receive his publication,
Ever Increasing Faith Messenger,
write:

Fred Price
Crenshaw Christian Center
P. O. Box 9000
Los Angeles, CA 90009

For additional copies
of this book
in Canada contact:

Word Alive
P. O. Box 670
Niverville, Manitoba
CANADA R0A 1E0

Harrison House Vision

Proclaiming the truth and power
Of the Gospel of Jesus Christ
With excellence;

Challenging Christians to
Live victoriously,
Grow spiritually,
Know God intimately.